Confederate Women

COVER ART: "A Night on the Battlefield" by Oregon Wilson. It depicts a true incident following the Battle of Third Winchester. On the night of September 19, 1864, a young lady named Tilly Russell searched the battlefield for wounded. She came across twenty year old Captain Randolph Ridgely of General Ramseur's staff, Army of Northern Virginia. Miss Russell sat all night, holding the young officer and staunching a bleeding wound, until morning when help arrived. (Courtesy of Handley Library, Winchester, VA.)

Confederate Women

by

Dr. Anne J. Bailey	*Mauriel Phillips Joslyn*
Dr. William H. Baria	*Norma Jean Perkins*
James A. Buttimer	*June Murray Wells*
Jeanne M. Christie	*Julieanna Williams*
Barbara Duffey	

Edited by
Mauriel Phillips Joslyn

PELICAN PUBLISHING COMPANY
Gretna 2004

First edition, 1996
First Pelican edition, 2004

First published by Southern Heritage Press as
Valor and Lace: The Roles of Confederate Women 1861-1865
Published by arrangement with the author by
Pelican Publishing Company, Inc., 2004

The word "Pelican" and the depiction of a pelican are trademarks
of Pelican Publishing Company, Inc., and are registered in the
U.S. Patent and Trademark Office.

Library of Congress Cataloging-in-Publication Data
Confederate women/ [compiled] by Mauriel Phillips Joslyn.
    p. cm.
"First published by Southern Heritage Press as Valor and Lace: the roles of Confederate women 1861-1865"--T.p. verso. Includes bibliographical references.
    ISBN 1-58980-186-5 (pbk. : alk. paper)
    1. United States--History--Civil War, 1861-1865--Women.--2. Women--Confederate States of America--History. 3. Confederate States of America--History. 4. Confederate States of America--Social conditions. 5. United States--History--Civil War, 1861-1865--Social aspects. I. Joslyn, Mauriel, 1955- II. Title.
    E628 .V35 2004
    973.7'13'082--dc22

2003018912

Printed in Canada
Published by Pelican Publishing Company, Inc.
1000 Burmaster Street, Gretna, Louisiana 70053

"To the Women of the Confederacy whose fidelity, whose purity, whose courage, whose gentle genius in love and in counsel, kept home secure, and family a school of virtue, the State a Court of virtue; who made war a season of heroism, and peace a time of healing. The guardians of our tranquility and strength."

Woodrow Wilson
Dedication of Monument to
the Women of the South
Rome, Georgia March 10, 1910

CONTENTS

INTRODUCTION

This is first and foremost a story about the various roles filled by Confederate women during The War for Southern Independence. In spite of the constraints of their traditional roles in southern society, they not only served as nurse and caretaker but also as spy, prisoner for their cause and even soldier. This then is their story.

To empathize with the women who experienced the War Between the States from the Confederate perspective, we must understand their place in 19th century society. In this regard, their role is almost universal. Women had the unique perspective of being more or less spectators of their world, while men ruled and made the decisions. When war came, Southern women found themselves observers in a patriarchal society — missing its patriarchs. The men had all been removed to the path of war. Perhaps because of their previous "observer role" those women were able to recognize quickly what was lacking in society. When war came, it brought the opportunity to act on these observations, step in with efficiency and fill very competently many roles which were previously nonexistent.

The ten women presented here have been chosen because they so well represent the role of many. With the exception of Loreta Valezquez, most have been remaindered to history's shelves in obscurity. The difficulty associated with finding documentation on women of the period makes it rare to write a complete story of an individual's experience. One historian stated that a woman was mentioned only three times in her life—when she was born, when she married, and when she died. There is some truth in this. Unless she kept a diary, or letters were preserved, there is little record of the average woman, unless she is mentioned indirectly because she was married to a prominent husband.

What has been attempted here is to gather stories of women not particularly the wealthiest or most socially prominent, of their time. The roles represented vary, but have common threads—the patriotic love of country, faith in God, and dedication to family. The independent women of today feel they are the first to challenge and achieve an equality in a male-oriented society. But Confederate women proved themselves capable. They drew from a remarkable inner strength—with no assistance from therapists or support groups. One impression these stories successfully refute is the myth that Southern women were largely social ornaments, male-dominated and poorly educated intellectually. On the contrary, they ran the country's day-to-day existence, and were accepted as capable and equal by such authority figures as generals and politicians.

One cannot read of Ella Newsom's relationships with the Confederate high Command and think anything but that she was truly treated as an equal, whose opinion was valued in regard to the good of the army.

If courage may be considered a term largely applied to men on a battlefield, consider the quiet courage of Mary Terry who endured the discomfort of a federal prison for her beliefs and refusal to abandon principles. The courage required of these women is no less the degree required of their male counterparts on the field.

There's a different kind of emotional courage found in the love of Charlotte Branch as a mother, and Susan Tarleton as a fiancee. Charlotte watched her most prized possessions—her sons—sacrificed and endangered for four years. Susan Tarleton was a young bride-to-be with everything before her, until the tragic news arrived that her future had been destroyed needlessly before the ditches at Franklin. We can only imagine the heartbreak thousands of mothers, lovers, and wives faced daily.

Adventurous roles also presented themselves, and were filled, by women such as Loreta Velazquez who "went for a soldier", and the homefront girls of the Nancy Harts.

The willingness to pitch in and sacrifice is evident in the successful "war work" of the ladies' aid societies. It is reminiscent of the more recent World War II USO, and canteens for the troops of the 1940s.

Finally, some roles reached beyond the war years to record the turbulent times, and keep memory of those lost alive. These we represent with Margaret Junkin Preston as the poet, and Mary Amarinthis Snowden and her dedication to Confederate Memorial Day, and the remembrance of who and what was sacrificed.

The female contributions may seem neglected to us in our reading today, but they were not overlooked as long as the veterans of the Confederate Army were alive. Monuments were erected to the Women of the South in several states. Poems were written, and incidents recounted which left lasting impressions on the minds of young suffering soldiers. Perhaps one verse from Albert Sidney Morton's poem "Women of the South" sums it up best:

> Who bade us go with smiling tears?
> Who scorned the renegade?
> Who, silencing their trembling fears,
> Watched, cheered, then wept and prayed?
> Who nursed our wounds with tender care,
> And then when all was lost,
> Who lifted us from our despair?
> And counted not the cost?
> THE WOMEN OF THE SOUTH.

What can we take away from these individual stories to give us new perspective and understanding? We cannot fail to be inspired by their examples as role models, and we can admire their compassion, suffering and eventual survival during the crucible in both their lives and our nation's history. These traits are still pertinent even into this millennium, reminding us that they are timeless virtues.

Charlotte Sawyer Branch
Date Unknown

1

THE MOTHER:
CHARLOTTE S. BRANCH
"The Mother of the Oglethorpe Light Infantry"

By
Mauriel P. Joslyn

On April 10, 1861, only days before Fort Sumter found its place in history, a 46-year old widow sat down to write a reply to a letter from her oldest son:

"I am satisfied now that there will be war and if there is, I would not have the slightest obstacle in the way to prevent my sons from going where duty called them, no not if my heart should brake."[1] The recipient of the letter, John Branch, was 23 years old, a newly commissioned lieutenant in the distinguished Savannah militia company, the Oglethorpe Light Infantry. He was then at Fort Pulaski in the mouth of the Savannah River, a part of the troops who had occupied the fort in January 1861. Two younger brothers, Sanford age 21, and Hamilton age 18, had also enlisted in the company. Their mother, Charlotte Sawyer Branch, was about to send them off to battle with her blessings.

Charlotte was born in 1814, the only child of Sarah McDevit and Walker Colburn Sawyer. Sarah McDevit had come to America from Ireland, and married Walker Sawyer, a New Hampshire sailor. When Charlotte was four years old, her father died at sea, leaving his family to make their own way in the world. So Charlotte became acquainted with adversity at an early age. Little is known of her childhood. Her education was typical of the children of her social class. She wrote a short letter to her son upon his inquiry about the infamous 1854 yellow fever epidemic. Her reply gives us a glimpse of her life as a child:

> I was a very little child when the Yellow Fever raged in Sav. in 1820. (it was caused by the dreadful rains after the great fire when so large a portion of the citty was laid in ruins.) Many of the buildings had deep

cellars in which were large quantities of vegatable matter which had been partially burned the rains filled these cellars and rotted the contents of them which [generated] feaver, that I have heard from the old Folks who new all about it. I was born in this citty and never saw a case of Yellow Fever until the summer of 1854, when we had it in Savannah as an Epidemic for the first time in my recolections (when I was about 11 years of age I remember that it raged there were 8 cases in full near where I went to school but I did not think any one was alarmed about it as we all attended school as usual) I know severall families who did not have a single case of Yellow fever during the persistence of that disease in 1854. Sarah Cornwell's and severall others had black vomit who recovered and are still liveing—.[2]

She grew up with her mother's perseverance to survive, and a talent for dressmaking as an avocation. A strong independent nature emerged which would serve her well in life.

The mother and daughter made a good living in the milinery business. It was Savannah's Golden Age in the 1830s, and many newcomers arrived in the city. Among them was a young Rhode Islander who had come South to seek his fortune in Savannah's commercial prosperity, and in March of 1837, Charlotte and John Henry Selah Branch were married.

To this union were born three sons. John Lufburrow was born on March 4, 1838, Sanford Walker on March 17, 1840, and Hamilton McDevit on March 17, 1843. It was a happy family, and John Branch's dry goods store made a comfortable living.[3]

Then tragedy struck an early blow. John Branch died in 1846, at the age of 45, leaving Charlotte widowed with three little boys, the oldest of whom was only 10 years. She raised them with the help of her mother, providing a loving home and nurturing environment in an extended family atmosphere. Central to this was her Presbyterian faith that God would never give her anything she could not handle.

Widowed, Charlotte once again joined her mother in the milinery business. She was an active church member of Independent Presbyterian, and the boys were well behaved. They were the light of her life, and everyone commented on the happiness and pride they obviously brought their mother.[4]

John, as the oldest, was given preference for an education, and sent away to school in 1850. Charlotte instilled in him a keen sense of duty as the elder brother. "When I look at you and think what a responsable situation you are placed in (that of an older brother) I allmost tremble for you," she wrote him at school. "I know it is an arduous one, but then think what an honour to be guide to your two dear little brothers. What a comefort when you are a man (if God should spare your life) to think you have never set them a bad example."[5]

In 1853, John entered the newly established Georgia Military Institute at Marietta, as a freshman cadet. His subjects were mathematics and engineering studies, to ensure a good job future. His younger brothers continued their education in the public schools of Savannah, at Chatham Academy. Though not given the opportunities that John received, Santy and Hammie were intelligent, hard working boys.[6]

Charlotte kept them on the straight and narrow path between good and evil. Her letters to John while he was away at school, continually remind him about responsibility, "to govern his passions," and "remember the eye of God is on you in every place." His behavior as a role model was constantly stressed. Through a mother's love and guidance, her fatherless children learned the meaning of honor, duty, principles — and love.[7]

In 1861, Charlotte was still the owner of a successful millinery business, in the three story house at 180 Broughton Street, enjoying much happiness with her boys, all three nearly grown to manhood. John had joined the Oglethorpe Light Infantry, a popular militia company, in 1855. He was employed in the office of Padelford, Fay and Co., a cotton factor on Bay Street. Sanford, also in the O.L.I., worked as a druggist's clerk on Broughton Street, and baby brother Hamilton was a clerk at a shoe store.[8]

Then the war came—in a feverish frenzy. When the Oglethorpe Light Infantry joined the Confederate Army, they were sent to the theatre of war in Virginia, and became Co. B, 8th Georgia Volunteer Infantry. Hamilton joined his brothers, and all three left their widowed mother.

Ever the doting mother, Charlotte worried and fretted that her influence could not survive the long distance separation. On July 15 she wrote to Sanford:

> Mr. and Mrs. Hine will leve on Wednesday for Virginia—I envey them. I believe I am the only [Mother] who can't do as I would like. I wish I could be with you my own dear boys. I would be so much use. I could keep your clothes in order and make your meals so much better....I hope you are able to keep clean as I have just had a terrible account of the want of cleanliness in some of the regiments. It is worrying me for fear that you are suffering for want of change of apparel.[9]

Charlotte threw herself into the activities of the various relief organizations formed by the women of Savannah to supply the soldiers she had sent to the front. Sewing circles met to make shirts, uniforms, socks and underclothing. Charlotte provided a quantity of blue checked material to make shirts for the company. She sewed four uniforms herself, and sent them along in a large box of provisions.[10]

While the company was stationed in Virginia, John was promoted to Adjutant of the 8th Georgia. This necessitated buying a horse, and John was unable to obtain the funds. Charlotte borrowed enough money from a family friend to acquire the necessary mount for her officer son.[11]

The 8th was ordered into battle at First Manassas on July 21, 1861, with all three Branch boys engaged. They were in the thickest of the fighting, where John was killed, Sanford taken prisoner, and Hamilton left to deal with the aftermath. He immediately telegraphed his mother with the sad tidings.[12]

Charlotte was one of the first to receive the devastating news that every mother dreads. By the evening of July 22, she was on her way to Virginia by train, hoping desperately there was some mistake. When she arrived in Richmond, she pleaded for transportation to the battlefield, but General P.G.T. Beauregard had ordered no civilians be allowed to pass. Heartsick, she decided to stay with friends in Richmond for several days, where she was finally contacted by Hamilton. She set out to find him in camp near Manassas.[13]

Arriving at the hastily organized camp of the 8th Georgia, Charlotte was shocked by the state of things. The boys who had led such sheltered lives in Savannah were now dying, alone and far from home, of disease and wounds. She stayed with them, nursing some back to health, including her own son Hamilton, while she wrote letters attempting to learn some news of Sanford who had been captured. It was here that she earned her nickname, "The Mother of the Oglethorpe Light Infantry", staying for months while she made arrangements to have her oldest son John's remains disinterred and taken home.[14]

From her quarters at Bristoe Station, Charlotte wrote her son Hamilton on August 26, "I spent a dreadful night. It is so terable to see so many sick. Mrs. Bayard's nephew was very low and is near...They buried 2 the morning we left. they died during the night. disease in camp is dreadful, dreadful everywhere but worse there, with not a comfort around them, so little attention."[15]

While she tended others, her grief over her own sons was carried inside. Letters of condolence arrived at her temporary shelter, and remembrances of John's character were summed up by a family friend. "If ever Savannah owned a young man of whom she might be justly proud, it was John Branch," wrote Correline West. "For purity, industry, valor, truth and chivalry, surely of him most truly it might be said None saw him but to praise, None knew him but to love."[16]

With John fell five other Savannah boys, all acquaintances. One of the fathers sent Charlotte a letter after they visited the graves of their sons together. Heman Crane had a remaining son in the O.L.I. "Mrs. Branch," he wrote, "allow me to commend to your care and kindness my dear son, my only son Horace — should he get sick again while you remain near the camp take him and care for him as you would for one of your own dear sons and the gratitude of a father and mother shall be poured out in humble prayer...”[17]

Charlotte remained at Bristoe Station until just before Christmas when, heartbroken, she left Hammie and returned to Savannah. On December 20, Sanford was released from Old Capital Prison, where he had been held since July 21. His mother had never ceased to effect his release, contacting influential people in Washington, D.C.

But she had been unable to secure a furlough for Hammie. In February 1862, John's body was disinterred and returned to Savannah. He was buried beside his father in Laurel Grove Cemetery on February 9.[18]

Sanford was paroled and returned to his regiment in June 1862. Hamilton's one year enlistment ended in May, and he came home to Savannah. Seeing his mother's grief over John's death, and Sanford's return to Virginia, Hammie reenlisted in a local company of militia. The Savannah Cadets was composed of boys too young for the regular army. Hammie was a veteran at age nineteen, and was offered a commission as first lieutenant. He accepted so he could be stationed nearer his mother. The Cadets spent 1862 and 1863 at the coastal batteries around Savannah and South Carolina.[19]

The hardships of the war hounded Charlotte just as they did women in every part of the Confederacy. Shortages of food, financial reversals, and her continual sacrifices for her sons' comfort in the field became her daily struggles. Her mother died in October 1862, and with both remaining sons in danger, she refused to be idle. Instead, she immersed herself in war work, whether sewing shirts and socks, packing boxes of food to send to hungry soldiers, or nursing in the hospitals around Savannah.

Both boys were now lieutenants, but Sanford remained in the 8th Georgia. “You can see by the heading of this letter that we are in the Union again,” he wrote to his mother on June 28, 1863, from an army camp outside Chambersburg, Pennsylvania.[20]

When Charlotte opened the *Savannah Daily News* on July 6, she relived a nightmare. There had been a great battle at a town called Gettysburg. Listed under the casualties from the Savannah companies was “Lt. Sanford W. Branch, shot through lungs—feared mortally.”

Too distraught to stay at home, she once again set out for Virginia, and General Lee's Army. After arriving in Richmond, she began contacting officials for passes. She traveled to Staunton, then Winchester, and made her way to Bunker Hill before she learned that her son was once again a prisoner. He had been too severely injured to be moved from the field hospital when the Confederate army retreated. Every last ounce of her mother's love was poured into pleading to gain permission to enter Federal lines. She pulled every string she could, contacting Savannah politicians, and Confederate Army officials.[21]

On July 15, Brig. Gen. Alexander R. Lawton sent a letter to Gen. Robert E. Lee on Charlotte's behalf, with the following request:

> Richmond, Va.
> 15th July 63
>
> General
>
> I take the liberty of sending you this note by Mrs. Branch of Savannah Geo, whose son was seriously wounded in the recent battle in Pennsylvania — Mrs. Branch earnestly desires to reach and minister to her son; and her case appeals strongly to every heart — Mrs. Branch has given three sons to our service — one of them was killed at Manassas, another is now facing the enemy at Charleston, and I trust she will be permitted to wait at the couch of the third, who so much needs her services—I beg that any officer to whom this letter may be shown, will assist this excellent lady and widowed mother in reaching her son.
>
> I am, General, very
> respectfully
> Yr. Obt. Servant
> A.R. Lawton
> Brig. Genl.[22]

The request was denied.

Soon a letter was received reassuring her that Sanford would live. She would not see him again for eighteen months, while he spent the harshest part of his experience as a Confederate soldier—in Yankee prisons.

Charlotte returned to Georgia, where Hamilton was still doing duty around Savannah. When Union Maj. Gen. William T. Sherman invaded the state in May 1864, Hamilton's regiment was sent to Dalton, where the Army of Tennessee would be the front line defenders for the next year. Once again a son was standing between the enemy and home. While she continued to seek an exchange for Sanford, Charlotte spent her days nursing in Confederate hospitals in Marietta and Atlanta, to be near the front.[23]

Hamilton was wounded on July 24, following the Battle of Atlanta. He met his mother at the hospital, where he received a thirty day furlough home. He and his mother returned to Savannah, but his patriotism would not let him remain out of action while his men were engaged. He went back to the army and was again slightly wounded in September.

Hamilton arrived back with his company just as the Army of Tennessee embarked on Hood's ill-fated campaign into Tennessee to attack the Union Army at Nashville. The Savannah Cadets were detailed as part of the army rear guard with the cavalry, under Gen. Nathan Bedford Forrest. After Hood's defeat, they covered the Confederate retreat back into Alabama, ragged, hungry boys amid the ice and snow of November.

The strain of the war and the threat to her family became more difficult to live with. Sanford was finally released from prison on December 5, 1864, after spending three months as one of The Immortal Six Hundred, held under the crossfire of Union and Confederate artillery. When he returned home, Charlotte was sickened at the change wrought by his ordeal. Underweight, nearly starved, and still coughing up blood from his unhealed lung, he was hardly recognizable as the boy she had sent to war. Three weeks later, Savannah fell to Sherman's occupation, and the quest for independence, in which the Branch family had invested so precious a part of itself, was lost. An especially cruel blow was the Union orders that all families of Confederate officers must leave the town. Charlotte became one of many displaced families by this act.[24]

Allowed to take only one horse and wagon containing what provisions were necessary, she and Sanford loaded as much as they could, and moved out into Effingham County, while Hamilton continued with the Confederate Army as it attempted to join Gen. Joseph Johnston in North Carolina. But he was too broken down in health to keep up, and arrived at the Confederate hospital in Augusta, Georgia in February 1865. Here he was quartered in a private house, and slowly improved. After a short time of duty sending furloughed men back to the army, he returned home in May. The war was over.[25]

The post-war years presented new difficulties for Charlotte. She had lost her home, her business, and her security. Nearly destitute, she was forced to join the Needle Woman's Friend, a society for the poor. Women sewed and mended clothing, and the items were sold as a charity for the makers. In this way, she earned a meagre living.

John's death had left an unfilled void in her life, but with a purpose. It convinced her that the sons of the South must never be forgotten. She was among the founding members of the Ladies' Memorial Association in Savannah, calling the first meeting in 1867. Each year the graves of Savannah's slain were lovingly decorated, and memorial services held. July 21 was chosen as an annual day to commemorate those killed at First Manassas. Her two remaining sons also became active in Veterans' organizations, and with the reorganized militias of the Oglethorpe Light Infantry and Savannah Cadets. Their mother was never forgotten by the veterans as the Mother of the Oglethorpe Light Infantry from their boyhood. She was the custodian of their flag, which was kept in a locked trunk along with John's uniforms and sword. On each July 21, when the company mustered for their annual ceremony, they marched to her house with much pomp and circumstance to receive the flag. At the end of the day, it was returned reverently to the trunk of memories.[26]

Charlotte Branch never attained any notable fame in her state, or even in her hometown. She died at age 80, from a fall in her bedroom, still beloved by the men who remembered her sacrifices during the war. But perhaps more than any women whose diaries are now well-known, or deeds recounted, she represents the majority. Like thousands of Southern women, she sent to the war her most prized possessions—her sons.

The Branch Brothers on the eve of war, probably taken in the winter of 1860-61. L-R : John, Hamilton, and Sanford

Notes

[1] Margaret Branch Sexton Letters. Ms. 25, Box 1-4. Hargrett Library. University of Georgia, Athens.

[2] Ibid. Undated letter of Charlotte Branch to Hamilton Branch, c. July 1861.

[3] Mauriel P. Joslyn. *Charlotte's Boys: The Wartime Correspondence of the Branch Family of Savannah, 1861-1865.* Rockbridge Press, Berryville, Va. 1996. 5-7.

[4] Ibid.

[5] Sexton Letters. Box 1, folder 1. Charlotte Branch to John Branch January 8, 1850.

[6] Joslyn, *Charlotte's Boys*, 8-10.

[7] Sexton Letters. Box 1, folder 1. Charlotte Branch to John Branch January 8, 1850

[8] Savannah City Directory 1860; Chatham County, Georgia Census 1860.

[9] Sexton Letters. Charlotte Branch to Sanford Branch, July 15, 1861. Box 1, folder 1.

[10] Joslyn, *Charlotte's Boys*, 21-22.

[11] Sexton Letters. John Branch to Charlotte Branch, June 14, 1861. Box 1, folder 1.

[12] Joslyn. *Charlotte's Boys*, 57-59.

[13] Ibid., 68-69.

[14] Ibid., 83-86.

[15] Sexton Letters. Charlotte Branch to Hamilton Branch, Aug. 26, 1861. Box 1, folder 1.

[16] Ibid., Correline West to Charlotte Branch, Aug. 29, 1861. Box 1, folder 1.

[17] Ibid., Heman A. Crane to Charlotte Branch, Nov. 27, 1861. Box 1, folder 1.

[18] *Savannah Morning News*, February 3, 1862.

[19] Joslyn, *Charlotte's Boys*, 157-158.

[20] Sexton Letters. Sanford Branch to Charlotte Branch, June 28, 1863. Box 1, folder 4.

[21] Ibid. Correspondence in Box 1, folder 5.

[22] Ibid. Brig. Gen. Alexander R. Lawton to Gen. Robert E. Lee, July 15, 1863. Box 1, folder 5.

[23] Joslyn, *Charlotte's Boys*, 291-293.

[24] Sexton Letters. Correspondence in Box 2, folders 1 and 4.

[25] Ibid., Box 2, folder 4.

[26] Joslyn, *Charlotte's Boys*, 445-447.

2

THE HOMEFRONT
For Our Boys – The Ladies' Aid Societies

By
Julieanna Williams

"The ladies of Alexandria and all the surrounding country were busily employed sewing for our soldiers. Shirts, pants, jackets, and beds, of the heaviest material, have been made by the most delicate fingers. All ages, all conditions, meet now on one common platform. We must all work for our country. Our soldiers must be equipped. Our parlor was the rendezvous for the neighborhood, and our sewing-machine was in requisition for weeks. Scissors and needles were plied by all. The daily scene was most animated. The fires of our enthusiasm and patriotism were burning all the while to a degree which might have been consuming, but that our tongues served as safety-valves. Oh, how we worked and talked and excited each other!"[1]

The South had become a country overnight; with no manufacturing, no workforce, and ill-prepared for war – much less all that it would entail to supply a sustained conflict. But the South would not be daunted. As rapidly as the men began drilling and forming companies, the women began preparing to send them off to war.

All over the Confederacy women filled with patriotic fervor banded together, with the resolve to support and sustain "the noble sons of the South." Women from all classes felt it their patriotic duty to serve their country by supplying the needs of the soldiers, with whatever it was in their power to give. Generously, and gladly, they gave food, clothing, medical supplies, and even their money. These women had no enlistment papers, and no uniforms to wear, but they heard the drum-beats, and the call to war.

Within a week of the firing on Fort Sumter, calls for aid were already going out. In Atlanta, one newspaper, The *Daily Intelligencer*, ran the following on April 17, 1861:

"The ladies of Atlanta are requested to form an
Association for the purpose of furnishing and preparing Lint and Bandages for the Army of the
Confederate States, now and hereafter to be in the
field. It is highly necessary…that this matter should
be tended to at once. The Mayor of the City is, there-
fore, earnestly requested to call a meeting of the
patriotic ladies…and that the ladies of our city cor-
dially respond to the call. 'In time of peace, prepare
for war.'"[2]

In response to the request, The *Intelligencer* the next morning
printed an answer from Mrs. W.F. Westmoreland, stating that "a portion of the ladies of Atlanta have formed an Association" and she
earnestly requested all "who feel an interest in the cause" meet at her
home "today," stating that "unbleached homespun, from 6 to 8 cents
per yard, is the proper material for bandages." She then asked that
no less than six yards be brought, because that was to be the length
of each bandage.[3]

In Nashville, "some three hundred ladies" assembled to
organize an association. Offices were elected, a "Mrs. Jas. K. Polk
was made President," and committees on "resolutions" and "organization" were appointed. The paper failed to give the name of this
newly formed group of patriots, but did state that they "then raised
nearly $1,000 to advance the objects of the association."[4]

Ladies' aid societies sprang up in virtually all the cities and
towns of the South. In the spring of 1861 enthusiasm and zeal were
in high gear. Materials were still plentiful, and quantities of uniforms,
shirts, socks and even undergarments were being rapidly turned out
by the industry of these ladies' groups. All efforts were focused on the
needs of the soldiers. Communities even pledged aid to the soldiers'
families while they were off to war. Everyone felt the soldiers wouldn't
be gone that long. "The war will be over soon," or so they thought.

As the ladies began formally organizing, electing officers
and writing their resolutions, the work continued at a feverish pace.
There was no time to be lost. Advertisements were being posted in

the newspapers, requesting help in cutting and sewing uniforms for whole companies. Realizing the acute need of funds to purchase what could not be made, they also sought donations for greatly needed medical supplies, and even gave from their own supplies of food and medicines, so that "the boys" might have some comfort, and a taste of home.

The fact that so many of these societies had formal names, and were well-organized with officers, committees, and written procedures, proves the seriousness with which these women undertook their duty. The names varied somewhat, but the object and purpose was always clear.

Atlanta boasted several major groups, among them were the Ladies' Soldiers' Relief Society, the Atlanta Hospital Association, and St. Philip's Hospital Aid Society. Savannah was home to the Ladies' State Military Association, the Soldiers' Aid Association and the Ladies' Independent Soldiers' Relief Society. The other cities and towns in Georgia followed suit, with organizations of similar names.[5]

Throughout the Confederacy, Soldiers' Friend Societies, Hospital Aid Societies, and Soldiers' Relief Associations were in abundance. The enthusiasm with which they worked was equaled by their creativity in raising funds for the much needed supplies.

They organized bazaars, balls, auctions, theatricals, tableaux, and concerts, all to raise the necessary funds to further their relief work. In New Orleans the elite sponsored a bazaar in April, 1861, at the St. Louis Hotel. Among the items offered were jewelry, fine china furniture and groceries. Over $60,000 was collected. Sewing supplies were purchased and the ladies cut out clothing for the soldiers, then hired hundreds of poor women to do the sewing.[6]

Benefits were also held for the wives and families of the soldiers. The Atlanta Female Institute held a floral festival. Nearly 160 young ladies from the ages of 7 to 18 put on a program. They wore white dresses with pink zouave jackets, and "garlanded with flowers and evergreens."

The paper reported the "hall filled to overflowing." One of the scenes they performed was a reenactment of the bombardment of Fort Sumter. They had a bit of trouble finding a student willing to hold up the staff upon which the American flag was held. One young lady refused, stating "that's not the flag of my country." After several attempts, a thoughtful girl finally agreed, but only because it was necessary to the scene. The bombardment was carried off by throwing flower blooms to represent the bursting shells.[7]

The women of the "Lone Star State," although on the frontiers of civilization in America, prepared for war along with their sisters in the east. Mrs. Piety Lucretia Hadley presided over the Houston Society of Confederate Women. She had already led volunteers in fighting the yellow fever epidemics that were so prevalent in their area. A bazaar was held under her direction and the proceeds used to purchase material desperately needed for uniforms. The boxes of clothing were then sent to the Texas soldiers in Tennessee and Virginia.[8]

Supplies of all kinds were being constantly gathered and sent to the hospitals and camps in Richmond where they were needed the most. There was much that the Confederate Government could not supply, so it was up to the relief societies and family members to do what they could to fill the void.

Kate Stone, a young lady of twenty, living on a Louisiana plantation wrote in her journal, "We were very busy Saturday and Monday packing the box for Brother and Uncle Bo. Besides the clothes, we sent quantities of preserves, cakes and other eatables that will keep." She continues her entry, noting that area ladies had also sent preserves and pickles, and that she was knitting a comforter (muffler) for a soldier that she didn't even know. A letter from her brother requested that something be sent for Lt. Floyd. "He is from Kentucky and can get nothing from his family, and no one has sent him a thing." Kate's mother sent Lt. Floyd a pair of gloves and socks, along with a note telling him that the food was as much for him as it was her own boys.[9]

The women that were in closer proximity of the encampments had the opportunity to visit the soldiers and take anything they felt would be of help. Mrs. McGuire, who lived outside of Alexandria, wrote in early May, 1861 that some families had already left their homes, fearing invasion from the Federal soldiers. She writes, "We who are left here are trying to give the soldiers who are quartered in town comfort, by carrying them milk, butter, pies, cakes, etc. I went in yesterday to the barracks, with the carriage well filled with such things, and found many young friends quartered there."[10]

Mrs. McGuire continued her writing and showed great understanding and foresight when she penned:

> "We are very weak in resources, but strong in stout hearts, zeal for the cause, and enthusiastic devotion to our beloved South; and while men are making a free-will offering of their life's blood on the altar of their country, women must not be idle. We must do what we can for the comfort of our brave men. We must sew for them, knit or them, nurse the sick, keep up the faint-hearted...There is much for us to do, and we must do it. The embattled hosts of the North will have the whole world from which to draw their supplies; but if, as it seems but too probable, our ports are blockaded, we shall indeed be independent on our own exertions, and great must those exertions be."[11]

Women that had not known "a day of toil in their lives" suddenly sprang to the cause. The wife of Judge Alexander Herrington, in rural Georgia, had thirty sewing machines brought to her home and "the neighbors gathered together and made leggins and clothing...Many and many days did she work with bleeding hands, caused by the constant use of the shears, for with her own hands she did the cutting for the others to stitch."[12]

No effort was too great, if something could be done to benefit the soldiers. Mrs. Susannah Oliver, age 79, sent in many socks and woolen shirts that she had made by herself. The shirts she had "spun, woven and made out and out, by her own hands." Mrs. Oliver then placed a written note in the pocket of each shirt. "Dear Friend: I sent you a flannel shirt; I trust you will be a faithful soldier to your God and country. Put your trust in the God of Battles. I hope you may return safe to your friends. (signed) Susannah Oliver."[13]

Work not only provided the much needed clothing and supplies, it helped calm the nervous, anxious spirits of those left at home. The prevailing sentiment seemed to be that "to be idle was torture." In Petersburg the ladies in the sewing society did not even rest on Sunday. "Sewing machines were put into the churches, which became depots for flannel, muslin, strong linen, and even uniform cloth. When the hour for the meeting arrived, the sewing class would be summoned by the ringing of the church bell."[14]

Spring turned into summer and the first real casualties of the war occurred. The ladies of Memphis informed Gen. Gideon Pillow, who was commanding the Tennessee troops, that "the ladies of their society" had a "large comfortable room fitted up to receive sick soldiers which needed nursing" and from there, "many houses are open" to which the soldiers may be transferred for private nursing.[15]

White women were not the only ones to work for the soldiers. The *Savannah Daily Morning News* reported: "The free colored women, actuated by the same public spirit, have tendered their services to General Lawton to make up one hundred suits of clothes for our brave volunteers and are...engaged at the work." Later, the paper even printed the names of the women who had done the work.[16]

Making clothing and bandages were not the only kinds of work done by the relief associations. In Milledgeville, the Ladies Aid Society "for a time made upwards of 3,000 "buck and ball" cartridges each day...these cartridges consisted of one round ball and three buckshot enclosed in small paper envelopes. The powder...wrapped in waterproof paper, was provided elsewhere." The Houston Society of Confederate Women also produced many cartridges, until the materials ran out.[17]

As the casualties of war mounted, new facilities were being "fitted up" in many aeas, to treat the sick and wounded. In the fall of 1861 the Ladies' Hospital was started in Petersburg, Virginia. The funds that were raised by a "series of entertainments" were originally to help build a gunboat for the James River, but the ladies were asked for a home for the sick and wounded, and changed their plans. A residence was donated for 12 months and nine rooms of furniture were given by families in the neighborhood. The community also promised two meals a day, and in 24 hours the hospital was up and running with 90 patients.[18]

The ladies of Savannah, who had been donating funds and supplies to the hospitals in Richmond, saw the need for one in their own city, and set to work to bring it about. A portion of a building at the Oglethorpe Medical College was offered, and accepted. They appealed for equipment and food from the citizens, and "to the Planters of Georgia we appeal for the donation of a few bales of cotton wherewith to make mattresses and comforters."[19]

While some of the supplies were now needed in local hospitals, many more were still being shipped to the soldiers in the field. The supplies that were received in the camps were always greatly appreciated, even though the women who sent them were seldom thanked personally. The thought that someone might be helping their husband, son, or brother was comfort enough.

A South Carolina woman told of her husband personally taking all the work of the Ladies' Ridge Relief Association to the camps. "He would go in a wagon with mattresses on which to sleep at night" because they had to camp on their journey. In a letter received by Mrs. Martha Ward, who was the "Secretary and Forwarding Agent" for the association, Colonel Butler expressed his appreciation for the boxes filled with hospital supplies for the Edgefield Volunteers, and called it a "very acceptable donation." He felt that because the soldiers knew that they were remembered, it would spur them on to "deeds of valor." He concluded by stating that "With such women we will be brave men."[20]

The Grove Hill guards received a box from one of their Alabama societies and reported that it contained, "60 pairs of socks, 25 blankets, 13 pair of gloves, 14 flannel shirts, 16 towels, 5 pairs of trousers, 2 handkerchiefs, and a bushel of dried apples." This seems typical of the boxes sent at this point in the war. The women had learned, for the most part, not to send "eatables" that would go bad while waiting to arrive at their destinations. Boxes would often include Bibles, writing paper, pens and envelopes or any other small articles the soldiers found hard to get.[21]

As the first winter of the war came on, and the Federals tightened the blockade, the price of all goods steadily increased. It became more difficult to fill the boxes for the soldiers, but difficulty only made them resolve to work harder. Women took their oilcloth table covers that had flannel backings and made coats out of them. Although brightly colored, often with sleeves and bodies being made of different patterns because one cloth wasn't large enough, these served as both overcoat and raincoat. Knowing the cold that the soldiers would have to face when blankets were needed and not available, carpets were taken up and cut up to be used as blankets.[22]

With great fortitude the members of the societies kept working along, while the pressures of providing for their own families increased. To keep the spirit up, songs were rewritten with new verses to fit the current situation, and patriotic poems encouraged continued devotion. The following two verses are from "The Southern Woman's Song," originally published in the *Confederate Scrap Book*:

Stitch, stitch, stitch,
Little needle, swiftly fly.
Through this flannel, soft and warm;
Though with cold the soldiers sigh,
This will sure keep out the storm.
Set the buttons close and tight,
Out to shut the winter's damp,
There'll be none to fix them right
In the soldiers' tented camp.

Stitch, stitch, stitch,
Swiftly, little needle, glide.
Thine's a pleasant labor;
To clothe the soldier be thy pride,
While he wields the saber.
Ours are tireless hearts and hands;
To Southern wives and mothers,
All who join our warlike bands
Are our friends and brothers.[23]

In February of 1862, the sick and wounded were beginning to pour into Atlanta, the winter had weakened the army considerably. Susan B. Lin wrote a letter to her young brother attending the Georgia Military Institute:

> "If you could be at home now to witness the suffering of our sick soldiers, you would not be so anxious to go to war. Atlanta is completely run over with them. Nearly every house in town is filled with them, I expect Ma will take them today. There is six or eight hundred here now and more coming every day. The City Authorities have turned the medical college Fulton House...City Hall, Hayden Hall...and the halls over the stores...into hospitals...The soldiers were sent here from Nashville, Murfreesboro and Fort Donelson, as they were in danger of the Yankees. I went...to carry them something to eat and I never saw so much suffering in my life...some have already died and others are dieing[sic]...They are well attended to, but they do suffer so much."[24]

The fact that the city was turning every available space into hospital facilities showed a resolve to adapt whatever was necessary to fill the current needs. Groups of ladies would meet the trains at the depot with baskets filled with food and drink. Tables were also set at the depot for the benefit of the soldiers passing through. The Ladies' Soldiers' Relief Society rallied to the cause and distributed "68 shirts, 75 pairs drawers, 18 pairs of pants, 6 vests, 9 collars, 72 pairs socks, 25 towels, 7 handkerchiefs, 5 comforts, old cloths, 15 bottle of wine, 4 bottles cordial, 5 bottles brandy, 8 doz. Eggs, hams, beef, butter, milk, coffee, tea, sugar, dried fruit, corn starch, gelatin, meal, grits, flour, rice, jelly, pickles, all-spice pepper, preserves, sage, etc." The society also kept up their contributions to the soldiers in the field. The *Southern Confederacy* paper listed 20 bottles of wine, assorted bottles of catsup, porter, cordials, honey, mustard, and castor oil, that had been recently sent.[25]

Contributions continued to pour in from groups outside the city as well. The hospitals received quite a variety of articles: underclothing, suits of clothes, socks, sheets, comforters, quilts, pillows, towels, shirts, linen, soap, bandages, rice, tea, sugar, pickled peaches, raspberry syrup, blackberry brandy, jellies, preserves, eggs, ginger snaps, dried fruit, and lint. Virtually anything that a soldier could eat, wear, or use was welcomed.[26]

The work of the women of the South was constant and undaunted, and of such magnitude that in April of 1862, The *Montgomery Advertiser* published the following resolution passed by Congress: "Resolved by the Congress of the Confederate States of America, That the thanks of the Confederacy are eminently due and are hereby tendered to the patriotic women of the Confederacy for the energy, zeal, and untiring devotion which they have manifested in furnishing voluntary contributions to our soldiers in the field and in the various military hospitals throughout the country."[27]

The war struggled on, and so did the relief work. The vast numbers of soldiers traveling caused the need for a new type of facility, and the Wayside Home was born. Chattanooga as well as Macon, Savannah, and Union Point, Georgia were some of the locations where soldiers, who could show they were absent from duty by "proper authority" would be given "a good supper and breakfast and a comfortable night's lodging." The register of the Union Point Wayside Home showed that during the war, over 20,434 soldiers, sailors, and marines partook of the Home's hospitality. The hundreds of soldiers fed "in the cars" were not even listed, although there were 12 Federal soldiers listed as having been fed. It was estimated that more than one million meals had been served from this facility alone. However, not all of the soldiers that stayed at the home were well and able to leave. During its operation sixteen "noble warriors" died at the home. Their passing was marked by a "Tribute of Respect" page for each man, listing his name, unit, and the date he died.[28]

Many women not only gave to the societies, but worked on their own at the hospitals as well. The thought that there was "many a wound to be bound up" and "many a parched lip in need of water" was enough to compel more and more women to the hospitals as the war progressed, even if it had not been considered respectable for women to do so before the war began.

A Petersburg lady spent several days working in the hospital and then returned home. "I appeared a few days later…bearing a basket of clean, well-rolled bandages, with a promise of more to come. The women had gone to work with a will upon my table-cloths, sheets, and dimity counterpanes – and even the chintz furniture covers. My spring-like green and white chintz bandages appeared on many a manly arm and leg."[29]

The hospital work and shipments to the soldiers were not the only projects that occupied the societies. Whatever need arose, there were sure to be devoted participants. The Ladies' Defense Association was formed in April of 1862, to raise funds for an iron-clad ship, which they accomplished, despite the odds.

Women not only gave money, but their jewelry as well. Even pieces that had been family heirlooms were put on the auction block. The organization did not confine itself to just raising funds however, but sought donations of "Iron railings old and new, scrap-iron about the house, broken plough-shares…and iron in any shape…will be thankfully received if delivered at the Tredegar Works, where it may be put into the furnace, reduced, and wrought into shape or turned into shot and shell." A committee of ladies also went to the tobacco factories, and the owners cheerfully gave up old available machinery. By July, the project was complete, and the *Richmond* was pronounced an excellent ship.[30]

As the war progressed, with no end in sight, and ever increasing hardships, some aid societies, of necessity, dispersed because supplies were scarce. Troop invasion, and the refugee status of women and families in some areas, caused other groups to disband. In many of these locations the work continued on a personal level, with the women concentrating on the soldiers in their family. There were still many groups of women that worked together with no formal name, acting only in the name of benevolence.

A young lady of seventeen, Susan Bradford, wrote of her experiences from her Leon County plantation in Florida. "We are busy spinning, weaving, sewing and knitting, trying to…keep our dear soldiers warm this winter. Brother Junius...has worn all his under garments to shreds and wants [us] to make him some new ones...I am spinning some wool into knitting yarn and with big wooden needles I have I am going to knit both drawers and shirts for him...I know the shirts can be knit, for I made some for father...but I am somewhat doubtful as to the drawers."[31]

Despite the problems, the major organizations were able to carry on through the war; especially those in the, as yet, uninvaded states. The Georgia Relief and Hospital Association, organized early in the war, helped equip four sizable hospitals in Richmond. Because the Association received funds from the state, and donations from private sources as well, they were able to provide great quantities of goods for the benefit of the Georgia sick and wounded in Richmond. Between October 1862 and July 1863 they were able to ship 9,270 shirts, 11,460 pairs of drawers, 6,340 pairs of pants, 3,331 pairs of shoes, and 1,867 blankets. Seeing yet another need, they also began raising funds for the relief of widows and orphans of Georgia troops.[32]

In the last year of the war the contributions slowed. They had gone from a massive outpouring in the early part of the war, to a slow and frugal stream, and a state that clearly showed the reality of the economic situation. There were still, surprisingly enough, some fund raisers and auctions put on. The necessity for soldiers' aid had not gone away. In Atlanta, even in May 1864, The *Intelligencer* announced a benefit concert on two nights, of The Atlanta Amateurs, a group that had formed during the war. "The manager takes pleasure in announcing that the Amateurs, assisted by The Brass Band, will celebrate their Third Anniversary by giving two of their popular Grand Medley Soirees." Tickets were five dollars, and each night's proceeds were to benefit a different organization.[33]

As late as July 1864, a new organization was being formed "for the purpose of affording all the relief possible to the wounded heroes of General Johnston's Army, who are daily arriving from the battlefields...contributions of vegetables and such other food as is best conducive to the health...are earnestly solicited."[34]

Relief efforts continued to the bitter end. Boxes were still being shipped, but the poor means of transportation could not always get them to their destinations, and many were lost or looted. One box sent by the women of Arkansas early in 1865 managed to get through. It contained many of the conventional items, but did include unusual donations as well: goose quills, home-made ink, and "stationery made from all kinds and colors of wrapping paper. Other offerings were corn-cob pipes with cane stems, and soap to keep the feet from blistering, in addition to "red pepper to keep them warm."[35]

In Columbia, South Carolina, with the city in turmoil, a bazaar was being held at the State House on January 18, 1865 despite rumors of invasion by Sherman. The House and Senate chambers were used to set up booths, and each were named after one of the states in the Confederacy. The tables were covered with damask and lace curtains, and decorated with evergreens. Emma LeConte described the scene at the bazaar:

> "To go in there one would scarce believe it was war times. The tables were loaded with fancy articles—brought through the blockade, or manufactured by the ladies. Everything to eat can be had if one can pay the price—cakes, jellies, creams, candies—every kind of sweets abound. A small slice of cake is two dollars—a spoonful of Charlotte Russe five dollars, and other things in proportion. Some beautiful imported wax dolls, not more than twelve inches high, raffled for five hundred dollars, and one very large doll I heard was to raffle for two thousand...How can people afford to buy toys at such a time as this!"

They had planned to hold the bazaar for two weeks, but would close it after only a few days because "Sherman's proximity forces them to hurry up." Almost one month to the day later, on February 17, the Federals captured Columbia, and by that night the city was in flames.[36]

Within two months Lee surrendered. The war was over. The relief efforts turned now from the soldiers in the field to the streams of veterans returning home. An English observer of the work of the relief societies during the war stated simply, "Were it not for the exertions of the Southern women, the volunteers would have been ill provided for." This was an understatement indeed. These were the women who sent off husbands and sons—often one son after another, as the war progressed—many of them never to return. They gave all they had "on the alter of their country." From privates in the service, to the President of the Confederacy, all were indebted to the courageous women of the South. A Louisiana Volunteer wrote his tribute in the register of a Wayside Home book: "Farewell Union Point. May the charms to others be as sweet, the influences encircling around thy rural bowers, to others prove as dazzling, and may thy beauties greet the coming strangers with the smile that cheered my lonely flourish."[37]

President Jefferson Davis spoke of the women, as he had seen them during the war:

> "The Spartan mother sent her boy, bidding him return with honor, either carrying his shield, or upon it. The women of the South sent forth their sons, directing them to return with victory, to return with wounds disabling them from further service, or never to return at all. All they had was flung into the contest…As nurses for the sick, as encouragers and providers for the combatants, as angels of charity and mercy…accepting every sacrifice with unconcern, and lightening the burdens of war…[these] dear women…deserve to take rank with the highest heroines, of the grandest days, of the greatest centuries."[38]

VOL. V.—No. 238.]   NEW YORK, SATURDAY, JULY 20, 1861.   [SINGLE COPIES SIX CENTS.
[$3 00 PER YEAR IN ADVANCE.

Entered according to Act of Congress, in the Year 1861, by Harper & Brothers, in the Clerk's Office of the District Court for the Southern District of New York.

Rolling Cartridges for the Cause

Aiding the Wounded

Notes

[1] Mathew P. Andrews, *Women of the South in War Times* (Baltimore: The Norman Remington Co., 1924), 75.

[2] The *Daily Intelligencer*, Atlanta, April 17, 1861.

[3] Ibid., April 18, 1861.

[4] Ibid., April 27, 1861.

[5] H. H. Cunningham, *Doctors in Grey: The Confederate Medical Service* (Baton Rouge: Louisiana State University Press, 1960), 141-42; Savannah *Daily Morning News*, September 19, 26; November 2, 1861.

[6] John D. Winters, *The Civil War in Louisiana* (Baton Rouge: Louisiana State University Press, 1963), 39.

[7] *The Daily Intelligencer.* May 3, 1861.

[8] Matthew P. Andrews, *Women of the South in War Times* (Baltimore: The Norman Remington Co., 1924), 416-17.

[9] John Q. Anderson, *The Journal of Kate Stone 1861-1868* (Baton Rouge: Louisiana University Press, 1995), 56.

[10] Andrews, *Women of the South in War Times*, 76.

[11] Ibid., 76-77.

[12] Rev. J.L. Underwood, The Women of the Confederacy (New York: Neale Publishing Co., 1906), 83.

[13] *Savannah Daily Morning News*, September 3, 1861.

[14] Underwood, *The Women of the Confederacy*, 78.

[15] *The Daily Intelligencer*, June 1, 1861.

[16] J. David Griffin, "Benevolence and Malevolence in Confederate Savannah," in *The Georgia Historical Quarterly*, XLIX (December, 1965), 354.

[17] James C. Bonner, *Milledgeville: Georgia's Antebellum Capital* (Athens, Ga.: University of Georgia Press, 1978), 158; Andrews, *Women of the South in War Times*, 418.

[18] Nora F. Davison, "Confederate Hospitals at Petersburg, Va." In *Confederate Veteran Magazine*, XXIX (September, 1921), 338.

[19] *Savannah Daily Morning News*, September 26, 1861.

[20] *Recollections & Reminiscences 1861-1865* (South Carolina Division, United Daughters of the Confederacy), Vol. I, 641.

[21] Francis B. Simpkins, *The Women of the Confederacy* (Richmond: Garrett & Massie, Inc., 1936), 23.

[22] *Recollections & Reminiscences 1861-1865*, 591.

[23] Underwood, *Women of the Confederacy*, 71-2.

[24] Letter. Lin Family Collection, MSS849, Atlanta History Center Library/Archives.

[25] Franklin M. Garrett, *Atlanta and Environs*, Vol. I (Athens, Ga.: University of Georgia Press, 1969), 531-32.

[26] Sarah B.G. Temple, *The First Hundred Years: A Short History of Cobb County in Georgia* (Athens, Ga.: Agee Publishing, 1966), 250-51.

[27] Mary P. Watt, "The Women of Alabama in the War," in *Confederate Veteran Magazine*, XXIV(May 1916), 225.

[28] J. David Griffen, "Benevolence and Malevolence in Confederate Savannah," *The Georgia Historical Quarterly*, ILIX (December, 1965), 355; Howard M. Lovett, "Macon in the War Between the States," in *Confederate Veteran Magazine*,XXXII (January 1924), 20; Thomas Spencer, Ed., *Wayside Home Register, C.S.A.: Union Point, Greene Co., Ga.*, copy located at the Georgia Department of Archives and History, Atlanta.

[29] Underwood, *The Women of the Confederacy*, 92.

[30] Ibid., 122-24.

[31] Katherine M. Jones, Ed., *Heroines of Dixie: Winter of Desperation* (St. Simons, Ga.: Mockingbird Books, Inc., 1990), 48-49.

[32] Cunningham, *Doctors in Gray: The Confederate Medical Service*, 143.

[33] The *Daily Intelligencer*, May 11, 1864.

[34] A.A. Hoeling, *Last Train From Atlanta* (Harrisburg, Pa.: Stackpole Books, 1958), 55.

[35] Simpkins, *The Women of the Confederacy*, 23.

[36] Earl Schenck Miers, Ed., *When the World Ended: The Diary of Emma LeConte* (New York: Oxford University Press, 1957), 12-13.

[37] Spencer, *Wayside Home Register, C.S.A. 1861-1865, Union Point*. Entry written by R.Y. Baker, 77 Regt. Louisiana Vols. Oct. 17, 1864.

[38] Underwood, *The Women of the Confederacy*, 20-21.

3

THE DEFENDERS
The Nancy Harts

By
Dr. Anne J. Bailey

In the spring of 1861, as local bands struck up "Dixie" at rail-road depots across the South, men kissed their wives and sweethearts goodbye. They were off for war. Patriotism, along with deeply-rooted state pride, aroused such feelings of loyalty that thousands flocked to enlist, impatient to join the fighting before the conflict ended. The southern volunteer eagerly embraced the future, and left home anxious for the adventure and camaraderie inherent to army life. The men would enjoy the esprit de corps that came with being part of an army, and could relish with pride the knowledge that they would take an active role in the fighting. Nonetheless, the soldiers' patriotic loyalty was often equaled, if not excelled, by the women who remained at home. As their men embarked on new adventures, women often felt the sense of frustration that resulted from being unable to participate in the nation's great drama. "We who stay behind may find it harder than they who go," wrote one young woman. "They will have new scenes and constant excitement to buoy them up and the consciousness of duty done," she sighed, while the women would be left to maintain the customs and conventions that defined southern society.[1]

Some women felt constrained and shackled by those customs and conventions, rituals so ingrained in the Old South that they defied challenge. Women could sew and knit, or provide aid to the soldiers in hundreds of small ways, but they could never shoulder a musket. Nevertheless, the simple phrase, "If only I were a man," adorned many a letter. While women could never openly wear the Confederate gray and march into battle alongside their men, they refused to renounce the right to participate, and one envious woman in Mobile announced, "the war is certainly ours as well as that of the men."[2]

Women of all social classes took on added responsibilities, but middle and upper-class women often had the most free time to reflect on their role. Refusing to be passive bystanders, a surprising number of educated women elected to demonstrate their patriotism by forming military companies. Drill teams appeared throughout the Confederacy, and for the first time southern women found they could participate in male activities without losing their right to be called a lady. They learned to shoot and drill and march according to William J. Hardee's *Rifle and Light Infantry Tactics*, and they did this with the blessing of, or at least without open objection from, menfolk at the front. These home guard units could be found in the North as well as the South, but generally, after the "carnival-like atmosphere created by emotions, not reason," had died down, most evaporated.[3]

Little is known about the women who comprised these military units; for after the war, as southerners tried to recover the old order amid the ruins of their shattered society, it may have been that few felt the desire to promote the notion that women had a right to engage in traditional male activities. Yet the story of at least one such company, the "Nancy Harts" of Georgia, survives. Primary evidence about this company, named for a Revolutionary War heroine, is scant, but there is little reason to doubt that it existed.Moreover, although the members of the "Nancy Harts" willingly became citizen-soldiers when the need arose, and continued to train for four years, after the conflict ended, these militia-women returned to the established roles that had characterized their antebellum lives.[4]

Much of what is known about the "Nancy Harts" comes from a speech given by Mrs. Leila C. Morris before the United Daughters of the Confederacy at Atlanta in 1896.Over thirty years after the war, the UDC emerged as the keeper of Confederate tradition. As a new century approached, the members passionately wanted not only to preserve but to further the southern view of the war. It was important to pass the "true story" down to their sons and daughters.Morris turned away from the glorification of the southern fighting man as she told the audience about the exploits of a group of young women. She also stayed carefully within the context of traditional femininity as she prudently harmonized the female traits of dignity and graciousness with the masculine image of carrying and shooting weapons. She believed it was important that the daughters could celebrate their contribution to the "Lost Cause" equally with the men. For women, like the men, treasured war stories that could be retold through the generations. She recalled how, at age fourteen, she had joined other young women in LaGrange, Georgia, in forming a militia company. Now nearing fifty, she introduced her topic to the assembled group with the claim: "Thus was organized, I believe, the only woman's company for regular military duty ever commissioned on this continent."[5]

Female militia companies often formed in girls' schools across the Confederacy, and the "Nancy Harts" was no exception since current or former students of the LaGrange Female Institute made up the roster of officers. The school had prepared its students to be wives and mothers, not soldiers, for one principal's motto was "to educate woman is to refine the world." Nonetheless, those citizens who had supported education for their daughters continued to support them when they decided to join together in a home guard; critics complained that women were losing their femininity by adopting military styles. In southern culture shooting had always been a decidedly male activity, but in both North and South, women became interested in learning to use firearms. This new preoccupation with weapons of war even prompted one northern woman to comment that she wished, "to God the war were finished," for she hated to see the "gentle-hearted ladies, admiring swords, pistols, etc. . . . ."[6]

The women who organized the "Nancy Harts" had very practical reasons for forming a militia company. When the war began, LaGrange was a particularly vulnerable location, almost halfway between the Confederate capital at Montgomery, Alabama, and Atlanta. Even after the government moved to Richmond, the Atlanta & West Point Railroad, which ran through the town, formed a vital link in the Confederate supply routes. Sometime during the early months, after most able-bodied men had left for the war, Nancy Morgan suggested to her friend Mary Heard that the women of the town organize a militia band. Heard's response was predictable. When, she asked, "Did you ever hear of a military company of women?"[7]

Yet it was these two women who organized the "Nancy Harts" with Morgan as captain and Heard as first lieutenant. They were typical of other women who enlisted in the militia. Morgan, born Nancy Colquitt Hill, was twenty-one-years old and married to a prosperous lawyer who became an officer in the 4th Georgia Infantry. Her two brothers, Miles and Joe, were also with the 4th Georgia in Virginia. Nancy was a cousin of soon-to-be Brig. Gen. Alfred H. Colquitt, and her husband eventually transferred to Colquitt's Brigade. Serving as commissary for the brigade, J. Brown Morgan was absent from LaGrange for most of the war, leaving his wife to manage the home and slaves.During those forty-eight months, Nancy lost her younger brother Joseph at the battle of Fredericksburg and another cousin, Col. Peyton Colquitt, at the battle of Chickamauga.[8]

Heard's story was similar. Almost twenty-seven when Fort Sumter fell, Mary Cade Alford had married Peter Heard a decade before the war began. Her husband, a wealthy farmer, owned over sixty slaves in 1860, while his mother, living with the couple, had about fifty more. Together Peter Heard left the womenfolk managing over one hundred slaves. And like Nancy Morgan, Mary Heard had a brother killed during the war.[9]

Morgan and Heard had been classmates in LaGrange, and they contacted their friends, many of whom they knew from happier days at school. Among those former classmates were Anne Andelia Bull (who also enlisted her younger sister Sally), Caroline Ware Poythress, and Mary E. Colquitt. Nancy Morgan also brought along her younger sister Augusta Hill and her young friend, Leila Pullen.[10]

These young women, who learned to drill and fire a musket, were not warriors.Indeed, gender conventions did not allow them to admit they might want to fight or be real soldiers, and even when they expressed their individuality in unconventional roles such as the joining the "Nancy Harts," they still had to behave like ladies. Nonetheless, they were middle- and upper-class women who realized that the time might come when they would have to defend their homes. They understood that with the men gone, no one remained to protect them from marauders from both armies. They did not seek to usurp traditional male roles, but when need arose to assume a man's responsibility, they volunteered. Perhaps they simply wanted to share their men's experiences. In most cases, however, it was a sense of urgency in rising to the occasion, not preference, that caused them to shoulder a gun. "My pistol is loaded," wrote a fellow female Confederate, "but, I trust never to use it, & never will except in self defence."[11]

Joining the "Nancy Harts" was a solemn decision for many women, taken in the light of the seriousness of the moment. For some of the younger members, however, the company furnished an opportunity to explore life in a way that society had never allowed.Escaping unchaperoned from the clutches of their mothers, the young women participated in activities that were considered "unladylike" without losing their respectability.

Moreover, although these women continued traditional female duties of sewing and knitting, many also became nurses. LaGrange was almost directly south of where Georgia and Alabama join the Tennessee state line, and as casualties rose in the region, sick and wounded soldiers poured into the town. Although the town had four main Confederate hospitals, families had to take in the overflow. "Each young woman had one or more of the sick and wounded to care for," recalled Pullen. "This meant [we had] to prepare suitable food and delicacies; to see that the necessary clothing, bandages and lint were always in readiness; to write their letters; to console and comfort them by reading to them from the bible and to divert and amuse them by reading light li[t]erature." Concerned mothers recognized the danger in allowing such intercourse between the sexes, particularly for young unmarried females. Pullen recalled that her mother took care that she "should not have charge of any of the handsome and dashing officers" by assigning to her a "private with a freckled face, carroty hair, ungainly and awkward, who was wounded in both arms and suffered intensely."[12]

But it must have been the sight of these young women as they marched through the streets to the beat of an old drum, banners flying, and guns propped proudly on their shoulders that both shocked and awed older residents. As Captain Morgan's voice cried, "Hep! Hep! Hep!" children "gathered on the sidewalk to see them pass, cheering lustily, and gazing at their guns and other military accoutrements with adoring and envious eyes." Morgan carried her grandfather's flintlock fowling piece, and Heard had a musket that her soldier-husband had rejected. The weapons, rusty from disuse, were often dangerous at both ends.Pullen, who dusted off her great grandfather's flintlock, remembered its "vigorous kicks."[13]

These female warriors were, however, not completely unchaperoned, for their instructor was a local doctor who had been found unfit for active service. Augustus C. Ware was also the brother of Caroline Ware Poythress. A young widow of twenty-six, Caroline told a soldier-friend how the group met twice a week for target practice. She had learned to clean her ancient musket as well as load and shoot it, both singly and in volleys. John T. Gay, who would marry the pretty widow in 1863, chided her from his tent in Virginia, "You say you can beat me shooting. Well, Perhaps you can, for I haven't fired a gun since I left home." Ware had family in the army too, and her brother Eugene was killed at King's School House in 1862, the first man in the LaGrange Light Guards to die.[14]

By learning self-defense, the women could defend their homes, but they had no desire to exchange gender roles. They drilled weekly, but they also maintained a lifestyle that maintained the proper male-female relationship. Many of LaGrange's young women visited their friends and relatives at the front in Virginia. In 1863 John Gay told his new bride, "Nothing would please more than to have you with me, this you well know; but to have [you be] the subject of all the coarse & obscene remarks, which, experience has taught me would be leveled at you at your every appearance in camps, would be more than I could bear, and I should be continually in a broil on your account." Nancy Morgan, who spent part of the war with her husband, had no such problem, and Gay continued, "Brown Morgan & Genls Colquitt & Gordon can have their wives with them and enjoy their society; But poor little Lieut has vastly inferior priviledges and could promise you but little pleasure were you to come."[15]

Gay was wrong. Officers did not always have an easy time finding housing for their wives. Although Nancy Morgan visited Virginia several times, she was not always able to join her officer-husband. In October 1863, when his regiment moved to an island near

Charleston, South Carolina, she planned to "take leave" of her comrades in the militia company and meet him. But Major Morgan told
his wife, "I have tried to make some arrangements for you to come
here, but have failed. . . . and if you were to come on you would have
to stay in camps immediately among the troops and I don't approve
of that. . . ." The menfolk of the "Nancy Harts" might support their
women parading down LaGrange streets, but they feared the criticism that their wives might receive if propriety were not followed.[16]

  With or without all the members, the "Nancy Harts"
marched, drilled, and continued target practice for four years. Unlike
militia companies, both North and South, that formed then vanished,
the women of LaGrange were still united in the last month of the
war when Union soldiers finally approached the town. Moreover, the
women had an idea of what to expect. As William T. Sherman
pushed through Georgia, hundreds of refugees had flocked to
LaGrange, and the horrifying stories they related became magnified
with each telling. Every Georgian could visualize the scenes of chaos.
As terrified citizens fled before the Union columns, recalled one
woman, "the face of the earth was literally covered with rude tents
and side-tracked cars, which were occupied by exiles from home—
defenseless women and children, . . . awaiting their turn to be transported by over-taxed railroad farther into the constantly diminishing
land of their love." Even after Sherman left on his march through the
Carolinas, Georgians never enjoyed a sense of security, particularly
those who lived in railroad towns.[17]

  The long-feared assault came in April, just a few weeks after
Sherman left Savannah. Federal cavalry, coming from the west, captured Selma and Montgomery. On the night of April 16, Easter
Sunday, a small Confederate garrison at the nearby town of West
Point on the Alabama-Georgia line defended the Chattahoochee
River crossings—twenty-eight Confederates died. With Union cavalry heading for LaGrange, the "Nancy Harts," together with other citizens, prepared for an assault. When the Federal column rode into
the town late Monday afternoon, they were met by local citizens,
including the militia-women, who had spent four years strengthening
their resolve for the day that they might have to defend their homes.

Were these women, who had learned to drill and shoot, "merely playing at war?" asked one historian. Or were they genuinely willing to use their weapons? "What terror we felt then!" recalled a member of the unit. They fully expected, claimed one woman, for "our homes to be sacked and perhaps our very persons searched by rude mercenaries."[18]

That question will never have an answer. There was no bloodshed, for the soldiers halted at the "sight of a brigade of girl soldiers." As one woman observed, "the officer in command of that detachment of invaders was a gentleman." When the column stopped, one of the Confederate captives told the Union colonel, "I have the pleasure of introducing you to a regularly commissioned officer of the "'Nancy Harts'." After quickly measuring his opponent, the colonel quipped, "I should think the Nancy Harts might use their eyes with better effect upon the Federal soldiers than their rusty guns." With that the women in the militia company "immediately abandoned military discipline and gave themselves over," as the city of LaGrange peacefully surrendered to Union Col. Oscar LaGrange.[19]

The "Nancy Harts" never fired their weapons at a living target, they never knew the awful sensation of killing another human being, but they were ready to defend their "homes and firesides by armed resistance if necessary," Leila Pullen Morris told the assembled Daughters of the Confederacy in 1896. Although their response to the crisis may seem extreme, Scottish born Kate Cumming had censured those who refused to contribute to the war effort. When a "young lady, . . . one of the handsomest women in Mobile," had complained that she wished she could do something to aid the soldiers, Kate scoffed, "I wondered what hindered her." While most southern women did knit, sew, cook, make bandages, or even raise money with bazaars, dances, and fairs for various Confederate causes, many others would have seconded Sarah Wadley of Louisiana who complained, "We young ladies are all so . . . useless." Or Amanda Chappelear of Virginia, who moaned, "There are none so . . . useless as I." Indeed, "What is the use of all these worthless women, in war times?" pondered another southern woman.[20]

The women of LaGrange never had to ask these questions, for they could always claim that by joining the "Nancy Harts" they *had* taken part in the war. Although their contributions may have been more of an attempt to examine their own sense of self-worth during a national crisis, they felt like active participants rather than passive victims.These experiences may have also helped encourage new confidence in their own abilities.But this chapter in their lives did not produce any lasting change in the social order of Georgians, for after the war the women of the "Nancy Harts" returned to the identities they knew best: wives and mothers. Most, however, remained dedicated to the "Lost Cause" until death, and as the war faded from memory, and a younger generation emerged, they sensed a need to glorify the "Confederate Woman." When Mrs. Thaddeus Horton wrote an article for the *Ladies Home Journal* in 1904, she celebrated the accomplishments of a group of women who had departed from their customary role, and had exhibited characteristics usually reserved for the menfolk: an interest in things military. In learning to shoot, these women had invaded one of the most masculine of activities. In a small way, Horton tried to justify those actions, thus she emphasized that while the "Nancy Harts" had been willing to fight, they had saved LaGrange from destruction by using feminine wiles, not weapons. The "girl soldiers" had accomplished their objective. "They did not fire volleys nor execute military manaeuvres," she firmly stated, "but they used methods equally effective: they stood between their homes and destruction."[21]

*** The author wishes to thank several people who made helpful suggestions to improve this article:Kaye L. Minchew and Clark Johnson at the Troup County Archives, Anastatia Sims at Georgia Southern University, and Daniel E. Sutherland at the University of Arkansas.

THE NANCY HARTS

Sisters
Sally Bull (Sarah C.) and Anne Andelia Bull

Sisters
**Nancy Hill Morgan – captain of the "Nancy Harts" and
Augusta Hill**

Courtesy of Troup county Historical Society

THE NANCY HARTS

Mary Heard
First Lieutenant

Leila C. Pullen (Morris)
First Corporal

Caroline Poythress Gay
*(dressed in black–a widow for the 2nd
time when Gay was killed in Virginia
in 1865)*

Courtesy of Troup County Historical Society

John T. Gay

First Lieutenant Company B, Fourth Georgia Regiment

John T. Gay married Caroline Poythress in 1863. He was killed at Fort Stedman, Virginia, just days before the war ended (quoted in the article)

From History of the Doles–Cook Brigade

Joseph Hill, C.S.A.
Killed at Fredericksburg, VA 1862

Two sisters in the "Nancy Harts"
Augusta and Nancy lost their brother in The War.

Courtesy of Troup County Historical Society

Major J. Brown Morgan
Confederate officer who served throughout The War while his
wife at home founded The All Female Militia Company for home defense.

Courtesy of Troup county Historical Society

Notes

[1]Diary entry dated May 26, 1861. Kate Stone, *Brokenburn: The Journal of Kate Stone, 1861-1868*. Edited by John Q. Anderson (1955; reprint, Baton Rouge: Louisiana State University Press), 17. The frustration that came with feeling useless caused many women to translate "this contempt into a fantasy of becoming men, a desire to escape from a gender identity that had in peacetime seemed entirely acceptable," points out Drew Gilpin Faust in *Mothers of Invention: Women of the Slaveholding South in the American Civil War* (Chapel Hill: University of North Carolina Press, 1996), 20. For more on role expectations for southern white women during the Civil War see Anne Firor Scott, *The Southern Lady: From Pedestal to Politics 1830-1930* (Chicago: University of Chicago Press, 1970).

[2] Kate Cumming, *Kate: The Journal of a Confederate Nurse*. Edited by Richard Barksdale Harwell (Baton Rouge: Louisiana State University Press, 1959), 39.

[3]Mary Elizabeth Massey, *Women in the Civil War* (1966; reprint, Lincoln: University of Nebraska Press, 1994), 27.

[4]The real Nancy Hart is the "backwoods heroine of the American Revolution." Born in Pennsylvania, she arrived in Georgia in the early 1770s. Her wartime exploit first appeared in a book published in 1848 although there is some evidence that there was a story in the *Milledgeville Southern Recorder* in 1825. The Georgia Legislature created a new county in the area where she had lived on the South Carolina border in 1853, and named it Hart County. Illustrations of her also began to appear in the 1850s. According to the popular tale, after Hart cooked and served a turkey for some Tories who had demanded food, she picked up one of their muskets, and aimed it at the men while they were eating. She demanded not only their surrender, but forbade them to touch the steaming food. The women in Troup County would have read about Hart's daring feat in school, for her story appeared in Elizabeth Fries Ellet's *The Women of the American*

Revolution, which was later published by George White in his *Statistics of the State of Georgia* (1849), and also in White's second work, *Historical Collections of Georgia* (1854). The story also appeared in George R. Gilmer's *Georgians* in 1855. Kenneth H. Thomas Jr., "Nancy Hart," *Dictionary of Georgia Biography*. Kenneth Coleman and Charles Stephen Gurr, eds. 2 vols. Athens: University of Georgia Press, 1983. Vol. I: 412-13.

[5]Morris, who was Leila C. Pullen during the war, was making a bold statement. It is true, however, that the "Nancy Harts" was one of the few female militia companies to survive until the end of the war. Leila C. Morris, "Personal Recollections of the War, Girl Confederate Soldiers." For more on the Confederate movement in the 1890s see Gaines M. Foster, *Ghosts of the Confederacy: Defeat, the Lost Cause, and the Emergence of the New South* (New York: Oxford University Press, 1987). Moreover, the South could not claim the only female militia companies for in New York City the police force drilled ladies in "sword and club exercises" so that they would "be ready to defend themselves in case of emergency." While northern society was not as restrictive on women as that of the South, the public was assured that these activities were acceptable under the circumstances, and the "nice little uniform" that the women wore was both "chaste and proper." Massey, *Women in the Civil War*, 39.

[6]There was another military company in nearby Macon at the Wesleyan Female Institute. Faust, *Mothers of Invention*, 203; Information for LaGrange comes from the LaGrange Female Institute 1850 *Catalogue*, quoted in William H. Davidson, *Brooks of Honey and Butter: Plantations and People of Meriwether County, Georgia* (Alexander City, AL.: Outlook Publishing Company, 1971), I: 240; Clifford L. Smith, *History of Troup County* (Atlanta: Foote & Davies Company, 1933), 129-30; Maria Lydig Daly, *Diary of a Union Lady*, 1861-1865. Edited by Harold Earl Hammond (New York: Funk & Wagnalls Company, Inc., 1962), 73.

[7]Mrs. Thaddeus Horton, "The Story of the Nancy Harts," *The Ladies Home Journal* 21 (November 1904), 14.

[8]U.S. Bureau of the Census. *Eighth Census of the United States, 1860.* Schedule 1 (Population), Troup County, Georgia. National Archives, Washington, D.C.; Henry W. Thomas, *History of the Doles-Cook Brigade, Army of Northern Virginia, C.S.A.* (1903; reprint, Dayton, OH.: Morningside House, Inc., 1981), 81, 84, 107-108; Georgia State Division of Confederate Pensions and Records. *Rosters of Confederate Soldiers of Georgia, 1861-1865.* Compiled by Lillian Henderson. 6 vols. (Hapeville, GA: Longino and Porter, 1955-1962), I: 563.

[9]U.S. Bureau of the Census. *Eighth Census of the United States, 1860.* Schedule 1 (Population), Troup County, Georgia. National Archives, Washington, D.C.; Forrest Clark Johnson, III, *Genealogical and Historical Register of Troup County, Georgia* (LaGrange: Family Tree), 1987, 131-32.See also Forrest Clark Johnson, III, *People of Ante-Bellum Troup County, Georgia* (LaGrange: Sutherland-St. Dunston Press, 1991).

[10]Davidson, *Brooks of Honey and Butter*, 244-45.The Bull sisters would lose their brother Gus in the Seven Days fighting; his body was never recovered. See also Keith Bohannon, "Gustavus Adolphus Bull," *Troup County Historical Society and Archives* V (June 1987), 2, 8.

[11]Virginian Charlotte Wright quoted in Stephen V. Ash. *When the Yankees Came: Conflict & Chaos in the Occupied South, 1861-1865* (Chapel Hill: University of North Carolina, 1995), 201.

[12]Pullen, "Recollections."Florence Nightingale's services during the Crimean War of 1853-1856 had added an aspect of romance to the idea of women serving as nurses. South Carolinian Ada W. Bacot, a wealthy plantation owner who chose to follow Nightingale's example, wrote from Virginia in 1862: "Every woman is doing som[e]thing to make the poor soldier more comfortable." Diary entry dated November 14, 1862. Ada W. Bacot, *A Confederate Nurse: The Diary of Ada W. Bacot, 1860-1863.* Edited by Jean V. Berlin (Columbia: University of South

Carolina Press, 1994), 165. For more on LaGrange during the war, see Forrest Clark Johnson III, "A History of LaGrange 1828-1900" (M.A. Thesis, West Georgia College, 198?).

[13]While the writers often use the word "rifle," it is more likely that the weapons were smoothbore muskets. Pullen, "Recollections;" Horton, "Nancy Harts."

[14]In a letter dated July 11, 1862, Gay told Caroline that her brother Gene had probably been shot by a member of the 6th Virginia Regiment. "There are in that regt some as cowardly men and officers as I ever hope to see. No brave man would ever kill a friend in that way." John T. Gay Letters 1861-1865, Nix-Price Collection, Troup County Archives. Thomas, *Doles-Cook Brigade*, 107.

[15]J. T. G. [John T. Gay] to "Dear Pussie," May 27, 1863. Their decision to marry rather than wait until the war ended came after he was wounded at Antietam in September 1862. On April 4, 1865, Caroline Gay wrote that she "once thought my betrothed dead, and but very few can imagine my feelings, but the good Lord was kind enough to send him to me and now I am his darling wife. . . . Jack, I believe I love you more and more every day. I think I commit a sin in loving you too much." Caroline Gay did not know when she wrote these words that Jack was in the hospital, wounded in the fighting at Fort Steadman along the Petersburg line during the last week of March. He died April 28.

[16]Brown [Morgan] to "Darling," October 15, 1863, Morgan-Hill Family Letters, Troup County Archives.

[17]Mary A. H. Gay, *Life in Dixie During the War* (1897; reprint, Atlanta: Darby Printing Company, 1979), 195. Also see Marilyn Mayer Culpepper, *Trials and Triumphs: Women of the American Civil War* (East Lansing: Michigan State University, 1991) for more on the refugee experience.

[18]W. J. Slatter, "Last Battle of the War," *Confederate Veteran* IV (November 1896), 381; George Rable, "'Missing in Action': Women of the Confederacy" in *Divided Houses*, 137; undated newspaper clipping, Mary Evans Curtright papers.

[19]Undated newspaper article in scrapbook, Mary Evans Curtright papers, Troup County Archives; Horton, "Nancy Harts;" Pullen, "Recollections." Oscar H. LaGrange, who bore the same name as the town he captured, treated the Georgians fairly, releasing the men captured in the battle at West Point to the temporary custody of their relatives. Colonel LaGrange later married a woman from Macon, Georgia.

[20]Morris, "Reminiscences;" Cumming, *Kate: The Journal of a Confederate Nurse*, 244; the last three women are quoted in Drew Gilpin Faust, "Altars of Sacrifice: Confederate Women and the Narratives of War" in *Divided Houses: Gender and the Civil War*. Edited by Catherine Clinton & Nina Silber (New York: Oxford University Press, 1992), 176. For more on middle and upper-class women see Scott, *The Southern Lady*. In 1922 there was another account of an address given at a UDC meeting. It was published as Mrs. Forrest T. Morgan, "'Nancy Harts' of the Confederacy," *Confederate Veteran* XXX (1922), 465-66.

[21]Horton, "Nancy Harts."Historian LeeAnn Whites points out: "While autonomy from their husbands and brothers also came as a wartime necessity to white women and children across the class spectrum, it cut deeply into their standard of living, forcing them to make constant sacrifices and to increase their labors without any real prospect of a fundamental alteration in their dependent status over the long run." LeeAnn Whites, *The Civil War as a Crisis in Gender: Augusta, Georgia, 1860-1890* (Athens: University of Georgia Press, 1995), 124.

4

THE SOLDIER
Loreta Janeta Velazquez
Alias
Lt. Harry T. Buford

By
Norma Jean Perkins

Was he? Could she? These are two questions that have vexed historians, as well as a few Confederate veterans, since 1876. Was Lt. Harry T. Buford really a woman? Could Loreta Janeta Velazquez really have disguised herself so well that even members of her own sex were fooled?

In her book, *The Woman In Battle A Narrative of the Exploits, Adventures, and Travels of Madame Loreta Janeta Velazquez. otherwise known as Lieutenant Harry T. Buford, Confederate States Army*, Ms. Velazquez relates many stories of her adventures in and out of disguise. This, say her critics, is where some draw the line.

One of her most vocal commentators was Lt. Gen. Jubal Anderson Early. He could not bring himself to accept that a woman could disguise herself as a man and fool any other member of her sex. Early saw it as a very negative reflection on Southern womanhood when Velazquez indicated southern ladies were "ready to throw themselves into the arms of the dashing 'Lieutenant Harry T. Buford,' and surrender without waiting to be asked, all that is dear to women of virtue."[1]

Who was this woman with the exotic sounding name? According to her autobiography, Loreta Janeta Velazquez was born on June 26, 1842, in Havana, Cuba. Her father was a diplomat born in Cartheginia, her mother was the daughter of a French naval officer and an American woman. Loreta was the sixth, and last, child in the family—three boys and three girls—spoiled, by her own account.

In 1844 the family moved to San Luis Potosi in Central Mexico after her father inherited extensive property there. Ms. Velazquez does not indicate if the move was to the city of San Luis Potosi or to the state of San Luis Potosi. It is, perhaps, an assumption that the move was to the western part of the state of San Luis Potosi based on events that followed the move there.

When war between the United States and Mexico broke out in 1846, Loreta, her mother and siblings were sent to the British West Indies province of St. Lucia where her mother's only brother resided. Her father became an officer in the Mexican army. After losing everything in Mexico as a result of the war, Loreta's father was bitter against Americans until his death. According to the autobiography, the family moved to Santiago de Cuba and the father inherited an estate at Puerto de Palmes and became engaged in the sugar, tobacco and coffee trade.

At Puerto de Palmes, an English governess was hired for the education of Loreta and the governess stayed until 1849. Loreta was then sent to New Orleans to live with her mother's only surviving sister to complete her education. In about 1851 Loreta was sent to a school conducted by the Sisters of Charity.

Based on descriptions in *The Woman In Battle*...Loreta read extensively on women in leadership/military roles: Hebrew Deborah who rallied warriors of Israel and led them to victory; Semiramis, Queen of Assyrians who commanded her armies in person; Tomyris the Scythian Queen took the field in person, outgeneraled Persian King Cyrus "routed his vastly outnumbering forces with great slaughter, the king himself being among the slain." "Bona Lombardi, an Italian peasant girl, fought in mate attire by the side of her noble husband, Brunaco, on more than one hotly contested field; and on two occasions, when he had been taken prisoner and placed in close confinement, she effected his release by her skill and valor."[2] "From my earliest recollections my mind has been filled with aspirations, of the most ardent kind, to fill some great sphere." [3]

It becomes obvious that the young Loreta was a girl with a very active imagination. One of her greatest heroines was Joan of Arc. With all of this in mind, when a young military officer became the focus of her attention, nothing could stop her when she decided to elope with him at age 14. Four years later in 1860 they were in St. Louis mourning the death of their three children.[4]

On April 5, 1861, Loreta and her husband celebrated their fifth wedding anniversary at the Commercial Hotel in Memphis,

Tennessee. The War for Southern Independence would soon begin changing not only the young couple's life forever but the rest of the country as well. Loreta's husband, William, joined the Confederate army when his home state decided to side with the South. An idea had already been formed in her head. She would recruit her own unit and give them to her husband to lead. There would, however, be one member of that unit that was a little "different" than the others.

It is to be assumed that because William had been an officer in the United States Army, he was thus qualified to be sent to Pensacola, Florida to train other recruits. Apparently, this was why Loreta was left alone to her own devices.

Loreta persuaded a male friend in Memphis to assist her in completing her disguise. He found a tailor willing to prepare the uniforms and other necessary clothing to fit the form that was designed to cover the fact she was a female. She describes it as being cumbersome and some revisions in design had to be made. Finally all was ready. She was complete with a mustache. She did make an attempt to learn to smoke a cigar and that almost proved to be a disaster.

Because Loreta was in Memphis, she decided to go across the river to Arkansas to do her recruiting. She describes going to a place called Hurlburt Station and a family by the name of Giles allowing her to remain on their farm while she did her recruiting.

A member of the Giles family, a young lady by the name of Sadie began to take an interest in the young Confederate officer Harry T. Buford, Loreta's new persona. While seated at breakfast on that first morning, Miss Sadie, wearing her brilliant yellow calico dress was becoming obvious in her attentions to the young lieutenant and her family began to tease her. Loreta heard her brother Frank "say to her, in a loud whisper, 'You need not stick yourself up for that fellow; he don't want you.'"[5] This only encouraged "Lieutenant Buford" to pay even more attention to the young girl.

Frank informed Sadie he would let her sweetheart Bob know she was flirting with the soldier and Sadie just turned up her nose. "It was not altogether bad fun to indulge in a bit of flirtation with Miss Sadie . . . but as I had matters of more importance upon my hands, it was impossible for me to make myself as agreeable to her as she would have liked me to."[6]

The recruiting effort paid off. According to Loreta, she enrolled thirty-six on the first day. She states that her quota was filled in four days including the two Giles sons, Frank and Ira. All two hundred and thirty-six men were marched to Memphis where they boarded the Ohio Belle for the trip down to New Orleans. The ultimate goal was Pensacola. One Thomas C. De Caulp was made first lieutenant and Frank Murdock second lieutenant in the new Arkansas Grays. Velazquez' unit has also been referred to as Arkansas Independents in her book.

Tragedy greeted the new company as they reached Pensacola. Loreta's husband was killed when a carbine exploded while he was training some men. Loreta was truly alone now. She left the unit in Pensacola and proceeded to become an independent soldier and going where she felt she was needed and could see some action. One battle in particular created a lasting impression on her:

> "At noon the battle was at its fiercest, and the scene was grand beyond description. The simile that came into my mind was the great Desert of Sahara, with the broiling sun overhead, and immense whirlwinds of sand rolling along over the plain between heaven and earth. The red dust from the parched and sundried roads arose in clouds in every direction, while the smoke from the artillery and musketry slowly floated aloft in huge, fantastic columns, marking the places where the battle was being fought with most bitterness. The dry and motionless air was choking to the nostrils, from the dust and smoke which filled it, while the pitiless July sun poured its hottest rays upon the parched and weary combatants. It was a sight never to be forgotten,—one of those magnificent spectacles that cannot be imagined, and that no description, no matter how eloquent, can do justice to. I would not have missed it for the wealth of the

world, and was more than repaid for all that I had undergone, and all the risks to my person and my womanly reputation that I incurred, in being not only a spectator, but an actor, in such a sublime, living drama."[7]

Even Velazquez' critics could not disclaim her obvious participation nor attendance in this scene. She goes on, "The fiercer the conflict grew the more my courage rose. The example of my commanders, the desire to avenge my slaughtered comrades, the salvation of the cause which I had espoused, all inspired me to do my utmost; and no man on the field that day fought with more energy or determination than the woman who figured as Lt. Harry T. Buford."[8]

Loreta Velazquez also known as Lt. Harry T. Buford, was not the only woman disguised as a man on the battlefield of First Manassas that day. Private Bill Thompson, of Co. D. 18th N.C. Inf., C.S.A. (also known as Lucy Matilda Thompson Guass) accompanied her new husband, Bryant Gauss. "She cut her thick hair close, took up seams in one of Bryant's suits, oiled her squirrel musket, and boarded a train for Virginia as 'Pvt. Bill Thompson.' . . . At First Manassas, an iron (shell) scrap tore open her scalp from forehead to crown (later protected by a silver plate)." [9] Miss Lucy lived to be 123 years old!

Although many people knew about "Pvt. Bill Thompson," no one sought to have her removed. For one thing, she was an expert sharpshooter and second, they sympathized with her desire to be with her bridegroom. However, her husband was wounded three times and was ultimately killed at Seven Days near Richmond. With his death, Miss Lucy's wartime service ended. Unlike Loreta Velazquez, she never revealed her secret to anyone until 1914.

Lieutenant Buford seemed to take a special delight in meeting an old family friend on the eve of the battle at Ball's Bluff. She said Colonel Featherstone of the 17th Mississippi regiment had known her when she was a small child. ". . . I was decidedly amused at the idea of renewing my acquaintance with him under existing circumstances."[10] Colonel Featherstone offered to share his tent in the event Lieutenant Buford had not been assigned quarters. Loreta thanked the Colonel and returned to her own tent where she informed her body servant, Bob, to make sure they were up at three o'clock in the morning and had plenty of provisions. This was, apparently, a signal that some action was about to take place.

Ms. Velazquez relates in her book of her service as a spy for the Confederacy. On one of her adventures, she returned to her female attire and, striking out from the Maryland side, proceeded to Washington:

> "On arriving in Washington, I went to Brown's Hotel, and having learned that an officer of the regular Federal army, with whom I was well acquainted, and who had been a warm and personal friend of my late husband, was in the city, I sent him a note, asking him to call on me. He came to see me very promptly on receiving my message, and greeting me with a good deal of cordiality, expressed a desire to aid me in any manner that lay in his power. I told him I was just from New York, and making up a plausible story to account for my being in Washington for any other purpose than what he would have considered a perfectly legitimate one, and consequently spoke without any reserve concerning a number of matters about which he would certainly have kept silent had he suspected that I had just come from the other side of the Potomac, and that my object was to pick up items of information that would be useful to the Confederacy."[11]

Loreta felt that the information her friend gave her showed he was not as completely informed as she thought or, he was prudently not revealing everything even though he did not suspect her of being a spy.

It should be noted that Ms. Velazquez fails to clearly identify a good many people she either served with as a soldier or sought information from as a spy. She did indicate this was to protect the reputations of some of those individuals. However, historians and even General Early felt this only tends to prove the incredibility of her story.

There are, however, a few people that support her claims. "I recollect another heroine, a Lieut. Buford of an Arkansas regiment. She stepped and walked the personification of a soldier boy; had won her spurs on the battlefield at Bull Run, Fort Donelson and Shiloh, and was promoted for gallantry. One evening she came to General Stewart's headquarters at Tyner's Station with an order from Maj. Kinloch Falconer to report for duty as scout, but upon his finding that "he" was a woman, she was sent back and the order revoked. She has written a book."[12]

There was some question raised on a plot to murder Lincoln with the approval of Jefferson Davis. "The witnesses to establish this charge—one of whom is a Miss Alice Williams, who was commissioned in the rebel army as a lieutenant under the name of Buford, . . ."[13]

It was apparent that for all of Ms. Velazquez' efforts as a spy, she was, like her friend at the Brown's Hotel, either not given the information she desired or she simply chose not to reveal this in her book. She was not discouraged however.

On returning to Memphis she indicates a readiness to begin it all again:

> "Notwithstanding many unpleasant things connected with this, my first campaign, however, I had certainly enjoyed myself immensely, after a certain fashion; for, to have taken part in two such battles as that at Bull Run and that at Ball's Bluff, and to have satisfactorily attempted a trip to Washington for the sake of finding out what they were doing in the Federal capital, were experiences that more than counterbalanced some which I could not reflect upon with equal complacency. If I returned to Memphis a disappointed woman in certain particulars, I also returned a hopeful one, for I knew better now how to go about the

work I had in hand; and as it was evident that some of the hardest fighting of the war was about to be done in this region, I confidently expected to have abundant opportunity to distinguish myself, both as a soldier and as a scout, and had scarcely a doubt of being employed in such services as I was best qualified to perform."[14]

Ms. Velazquez did not mince words when it came to describing scenes after a battle:

"In many of the trenches, especially where the fiercest fighting had taken place, the bodies were heaped together, six or seven feet high, and the faces of the corpses, distorted with the agonies of their death struggles, were hideous to look at. Those who fell, and died where they were shot, were comparatively fortunate, for their sufferings were soon ended. It was sickening, however, to think of the many poor fellows who, after fighting bravely, and falling helpless from their wounds, had their lives crushed out, and their forms mangled beyond recognition, by the furiously driven artillery." [15]

In 1876, a woman had to have witnessed these scenes in order to so accurately describe them. There was no television nor movies to bring the gore to the mind. Loreta writes about how the terrible sights affected her when they occurred but she still was excited to the point of being able to continue in her position. It was only later, reflecting on those scenes "that I fully realized what a fearful thing this human slaughtering was."[16]

New Orleans and Benjamin Butler; what a combination! Loreta discusses her difficulties in her former city of residence during one of her spy missions. It seems that she was in New Orleans to pass some information on to the Confederacy. She secured the friendship of a Yankee officer in the Thirty-first Massachusetts

Infantry and fabricated a tale of being out of the city in Carrolton. This was to be her cover.

She continues, in her story, that the unthinkable happened. The officer that she gave her dispatch to was captured. As luck would have it, some how or another, it was discovered that she had written the message; "[The] result was that I was placed under arrest, and taken before Butler himself."[17]

Loreta decided to match wits with Butler and beat him at his own game. Could this be possible? A woman making a fool of Benjamin Butler, and in New Orleans! It seems that Loreta had purchased papers indicating that she was a British subject. When she informed Butler of this and demanded not to be put under arrest in the Custom House but instead to be released to the British consul, he just laughed and said, in effect, he didn't have any use for the British. She was remanded to the Custom House.

Ms. Velazquez knew not only officers, a sergeant that she was acquainted with heard of her imprisonment and came for a visit. Through this sergeant she procured paper, pen and ink and promptly wrote to the British consul, Mr. Coppell. Apparently, her papers were authentic looking enough after the consul reviewed them for he met with Butler and the result was the release of Ms. Velazquez from her prison.

No one can say that Loreta was a slow learner. She knew that her spy duties in New Orleans had to come to an end due to her arrest and any suspicion of her activities. Loreta had to leave town as soon as possible.

New Orleans was not the only place with a jail for spies. Castle Thunder in Richmond was the next stop for Loreta. This time she was accused of being a woman in disguise and a Federal spy. A meeting with General Winder and she was back in business as a Confederate spy. Another near arrest in North Carolina. Time to move on.

Atlanta was the next stop. Here, Loreta learned that her brother was in the Confederate service and serving in the Trans-Mississippi department. She also learned that Thomas De Caulp, now a captain, was near Spring Hill with Van Dorn. It seems that De

Caulp was the apple of her eye and she was most anxious to see him. The last time she was with him was when they served together at Shiloh with Loreta disguised as Lieutenant Buford. She enjoyed the dual role and delighted in learning De Caulp's opinion of her as Lieutenant Buford as well as his expressions of love for Loreta. She wrote, "To have been able to fight by the side of my lover in one of the greatest battles of the war, and to be praised by him for my valor, were of themselves matters for intense satisfaction."[18]

It was not to be a happily-ever-after ending for the couple. De Caulp was wounded and even though they married, he died of his wounds not long after. It is interesting to note, Thomas De Caulp is the only one of her four husbands that she clearly identified. We do know, based on her autobiography that she married two more times after De Caulp and had a son by the last husband. Supporting the child (the husband had died) was the reason given for writing her memoirs.

Loreta Janeta Velazquez wrote extensively about a great many activities in which she participated or claims to have participated. On April 26, 1865 (Confederate Gen. Joseph Johnston's day of surrender) Loreta Janeta Velazquez, her brother and his wife and two children sailed on a Cunard line ship for Europe. She was tired. She had done so much. Time for a rest.

On visiting the Cathedral of Rheims, she reflected on Joan of Arc:

> "At the time of my visit to Rheims, however, I was of a more practical turn of mind than I had been a few years before. The romance had been pretty well knocked out of me by the rough experience of real life; and although I was better able to appreciate the performances of Joan of Arc at their true value, somehow they did not interest me to the extent they once did." [19]

There seemed to be a question on the morals of some of the women who disguised themselves as males for the purpose of doing their part for the Confederacy. Were they really there to fight for the South or were they there for profit/pleasure? Exactly what prompted these women can not be known by us. We have documentation of a few individuals. This gives us a minute number of women that participated in this critical time in our history.

Certainly, Loreta Janeta Velazquez has attempted to relate very personal and real experiences to us. Was she really a soldier in it for the excitement and challenge? Or was she only a woman of questionable character? It would have been easier to say the least, if she had given more precise dates and complete names. It should be noted, she never gave her own brother's name in the book when she discussed him with an officer in his regiment. She simply referred to him as Captain _____.

This was exactly one of General Early's arguments. He claims that she got some of the dates of the battles wrong. She explained that she had lost her journal and notes and had to write from memory. Without the research materials available then as now, she did a remarkable job. Loreta says she did not want to name everyone because she did not want to cause embarrassment to anyone, a very reasonable concern given some of the circumstances she was involved in.

Verification of the activities of Loreta Janeta Velazquez/ Lt. Harry T. Buford can be found in the person of Henry Birch, a *New York Herald* correspondent who was in jail with Loreta in Castle Thunder. During this time, Loreta claimed to be Mrs. Alice Williams. One interesting comment made by Birch was not included in Mme. Velazquez' book. He mentioned that after Mrs. Williams was released, she remained at the prison for several days "boarding, drinking, gambling, and carousing with Captain Alexander and the other officers."[20] Was this really Mrs. Williams (Loreta) or was it really Lieutenant Buford?

IN A BAR·ROOM IN MEMPHIS.

**Loreta Janeta Velazquez
or Lt. Harry T. Buford?**

Notes

[1] Sylvia D. Hoffert,. "Madame Loreta Velazquez: Heroine or Hoaxer?" in *Civil War Times Illustrated*, June 1974: 29.

[2] Loreta Janeta Velazquez. *The Woman in Battle: A Narrative of the Exploits, Adventures, and Travels of Madame Loreta Janeta Velazquez, otherwise Known as Lieutenant Harry T. Buford, Confederate States Army*, ed. C.J. Worthington (New York: Merrill 1972), 34.

[3] Velazquez, 41.

[4] Hoffert, 25.

[5] Velazquez, 83.

[6] Ibid.

[7] Ibid., 105.

[8] Ibid.

[9] Jay Hoar. "The South's Last Boys/Girls in Gray" in *Confederate Veteran Magazine*, May-June 1994:5.

[10] Velazquez, 117.

[11] Ibid., 138.

[12] B.L. Ridley. "Heroines of the South" in *Confederate Veteran Magazine*, April 1896:107.

[13] U. S. Department of War. The War of the Rebellion: A Compilation of the Official Records of the Union and Confederate Armies. (Washington, D.C.: 1899), Series II, Vol. VIII.

[14] Velazquez, 146.

[15] Ibid., 171-72.

[16] Ibid.

[17] Ibid., 259.

[18] Ibid., 291.

[19] Ibid., 524-25.

[20] Mary Elizabeth Massey. *Bonnet Brigades*, (New York: Alfred A. Knopf, 1966).

5

THE BETROTHED
Susan Tarleton of Mobile

By
Mauriel Phillips Joslyn

A wartime romance is like no other. The lovers know they defy the threat of tragedy that looms near them. The passion is more intense, the courtship short and reckless, in an attempt to cheat death and live a full life in a short time, aloof from the chaos around them.

The wedding party that gathered on a cold January 13th evening in 1864, was destined to profoundly effect each other's lives forever. Gen. William J. Hardee, age 48, was marrying Mary Foreman Lewis of Demopolis, Alabama. His best friends, officers from the Army of Tennessee, were on hand to witness and celebrate the occasion. The bride was the twenty-six year old daughter of a Greene, County planter, and the ceremony was to be at Bleak House Plantation, the home of her brother Maj. Ivey Foreman Lewis. The beautiful and impressive residence was like a scene from a dream— filled with European art, handsome men in resplendent uniforms, and a festive atmosphere that contradicted the usually straightened everyday conditions of a country at war.[1]

When William and Mary Hardee had said their vows, the bridal party and attendants prepared to depart for Mobile. They boarded a steamboat on the Tombigbee River, and for a 24 hour period the war was pushed into the wings, as the bride and groom began their wedded bliss, while their attendants became better acquainted.

As much as she tried, the twenty-four year old maid of honor, Sue Tarleton could hardly keep from staring at the tall, slender officer who had accompanied General Hardee as best man. She found his striking military bearing irresistible, his black hair and beard, with a hint of gray, distinguished. And when she was finally introduced to Maj. Gen. Patrick Ronayne Cleburne, and locked gazes with his merry blue, Irish eyes her heart fell instantly in love. The feeling was mutual. Her hazel eyes captivated him, and he instinctively knew that this was a turning point in his life. This petite and vivacious, strawberry blonde figure was the girl he wanted to marry.[2]

Cupid was hard at work on that steamboat. Among the other attendants who became romantically involved was Susan's brother Robert Tarleton and friend Sarah Lightfoot, while Lt. Henry Goldthwaite, whose cousin General Cleburne had cited for bravery in command of an artillery battery at Ringgold Gap, was wooing Susan's sister Grace.[3]

The next day, the boat docked in Mobile and General Hardee and his bride continued their honeymoon.Patrick Cleburne had taken his first leave since the war began, to attend the wedding. He decided to spend the rest of his furlough in the picturesque City by the Bay. Cleburne enjoyed the brief resumption of a normal life. He stayed at the Battle House, the finest hotel in town, and spent his days leisurely walking the bustling streets. But it was his frequent visits to the Tarleton house on St. Louis and Claiborne Steets, where Susan lived that highlighted his days. He was readily accepted as a suitor by her father, George Tarleton, a cotton factor and bank president from New Hampshire, who struggled to remain indifferent to taking sides in the war, despite his ardently secessionist wife and children. Tarleton had come to Mobile as a young man and married Margaret Brack, daughter of a prominent family, in 1837.[4]

The comfortable brick house at 351-353 St. Louis Street became Pat Cleburne's place to dream of the future, to share his thoughts and engage in parlor songs, good food, and a social life long put aside.

Susan was flattered at his attentions. Though he surpassed her age by twelve years, he was boyish enough to narrow the gap. As she got to know him better, her general became an enigma to her. This rising star of the Confederacy—the hero of Ringgold Gap— was almost awkward when alone in her presence, sweetly shy. As their days together passed, one by one, she realized she was seeing a side of this man rarely revealed to anyone.

His Irish accent was subtle but discernable, softened by a decade of life in Arkansas. Yet it became crisp and clear when he related his exploits, like the first encounter with a horse who proved too much to handle, promptly dumping its rider in a swamp, much to everyone's amusement but his own. Or when he admitted that he couldn't even dance when he first came to Helena, Arkansas, and had sustained much chiding by his newfound friends. But his brogue became most pronounced when he talked of battle—when his usually somber, gray eyes turned icy blue, a measure of his passion. She studied his handsome face as he showed her the scar from his wound at Perryville, Kentucky in 1862, now hidden in his jaw beneath a growth of black beard, and described with animated pride how his boys had stopped the Yankees cold in their tracks at Ringgold Gap, saving Bragg's Army.[5]

She listened, riveted to his stories. Could this quiet, gentle soul be the same that struck such fear in the Yankee Army? Whose very presence on a horse at the head of his men reminded them of a Celtic Chieftain of long ago? This man who spoke in such a soft eloquent tone of his childhood, and home in the "old Country" that it brought a lump to her throat was the same whose thundering voice rose above the sound of war, and moved men to throw themselves in the face of death itself to obey his orders because of the love each felt for the other, the leader and the led. Impoverished gentry fleeing the potato famine, Cleburne had crossed the ocean with not a cent to his name, and with no prospects as a young man of 21, had carved a life for himself as a lawyer in the American ideal of success.

This man, who had stood beside friends in fist fights and duels, was almost blushing as he asked for her hand in marriage. How could she resist? He had won her heart with his simple honesty and charm. Gen. Patrick R. Cleburne and Miss Susan Tarleton became engaged only days after meeting.

While in Mobile, Gen. Cleburne was asked to review the Confederate troops in the city with the commander of the Department, Maj. Gen. Dabney A. Maury. January 23rd was a Saturday afternoon few citizens would forget. A grand reivew of the troops was staged in honor of the distinguished visitor. Several thousand infantry, artillery, and cavalry participated, as pedestrians thronged the streets. Each regiment came to "present arms" as the generals rode by, and Sue Tarleton watched to catch a glimpse of her fiance through the crowd. The newspapers lauded him as a "soldier whom every true Confederate should delight to know."[6]

But all good things must end, and his furlough was nearly over. He had a photograph taken while still in Mobile, and presented it to his Susie on his last visit.She gave him in return one of her embroidered handkerchiefs as a memento. Saying good-bye was hard for both, but promises to write were exchanged, and be patient until his next leave. Within a week, General Cleburne had returned to his troops at Tunnell Hill, Georgia. His drastically changed life was evident to his men by the look on his face. His adjutant, Capt. Irving Buck noted the perceptible elation of his commander in a letter to his sister. "Gen. Cleburne says he had a wonderful time. Rumor says he lost his heart with a young lady in Mobile. He has been in a heavenly mood and talks about another leave, already."[7]

The cold North Georgia winter descended on the army camp. It was a quiet time, when neither side chose to pursue military matters. The long winter darkness provided little daylight for activities.

The early signs of spring brought with them another furlough for Pat Cleburne, and he returned to Mobile to pursue his romance. Captain Buck aluded to the General's leave in a letter home. "Gen. Cleburne expects to start on a twelve days leave this evening to visit his sweetheart, he has scarcely been back a month, this is very suggestive is it not? Would not be surprised at another wedding soon."

Cleburne indeed talked of a wedding date with Susan. Everything was moving so swiftly she was caught off guard, and seems to have stalled things a little before finally consenting.This only made her lover more determined. It was an idyllic ten days together. The couple took every opportunity to sneak off to quiet places in the garden, or moments together in the parlor. They went on walks and rides through town and the countryside. Every minute was precious.[8]

This short preview of life together appealed to Patrick Cleburne. Susan was his ideal of a woman. She was intelligent and accomplished in music and literature, the results of attending the Barton Academy in Mobile. This complemented her fiancee's great love for and knowledge of the English poets. They had much in common to talk about in this regard. She filled another void as well. He longed for the companionship of a wife, and a place within a real family, having been alone for fourteen years in a new and adopted homeland. He didn't know when his next leave would be, but they would use the time between to plan their wedding.

Cleburne returned to his command happy with these prospects, which he confided to his friends and staff officers. His absence from Susan was offset by their letters, and his duties in a winter camp. That he was relieved by her acceptance to be his wife is related in this letter to Sarah Lightfoot, whom he is trying to convince to marry Robert Tarleton, another couple in the wedding party, and prospective in-laws.

Battle House, Mobile
11th March, 1864

Dear Miss Sallie

I cannot think of leaving Mobile, the scene of so many happy memories of yourself and sister, without writing you the news. I arrived here last Sunday. I took advantage of the lull after the little storm at Dalton to come down and learn my fate from Miss Sue. After keeping me in cruel suspense for six weeks she has at length consented to be mine and we are engaged. I need not say how this has made me feel. From all I saw when we parted, I have little doubt but that you can without a very great stretch of memory recall what the feelings of an accepted lover are when the fair one has relented, when the heartless little conqueror shows that she is all heart by descending from her tall triumphal car, lifting her wounded captive from the mud and placing him palpitating with a thousand new emotions by her side....I must ask you to revert to your own experience again. You can imagine yourself the magnanimous vanquisher and some brave young fellow of our acquaintance the resuscitated captive. You still hold the reigns in your own hands. Alas! What can the poor captive do but go about in the flowery fetters wherever your will directs—over the uneven long doubtful road between acceptance and matrimony, weeks as long as months, months as long as years, must be traveled over in a dangerous conveyance which may upset and break the accepted's heart if not his neck at any moment; and this must continue until he succeeds in coaxing or snatching the reins from his bethrothed's hands. Once he can accomplish this he will answer your question by driving as straight and swift as an arrow to the altar and transforming Miss Sallie into a meek, obedient, exemplary, happy wife; and himself into such a pattern of a lord and master...And now, Miss Sallie, I shall expect to hear all your secrets and some happy day to be able to call myself more than your sincere friend.

P.R. Cleburne[9]

Robert Tarleton spoke of the consequences of this visit to Sallie, his future wife. "She is certainly quite happy and likes him very much indeed. I have not seen any of his letters yet but intend to make her show me some when I come up again. Mother says the correspondence is a severe tax upon Sue's energy. She says the General complains of the brevity of her letters and says she takes all sorts of advantages of him by writing very large and leaving large intervals between the lines."[10]

When a rare snowfall occurred in March, Cleburne enthusiastically joined his men in a snowball fight. The play took on a wargame atmosphere when some men belonging to another general in Cleburne's division actually seized cannon, and horses and joined the fray. Cleburne's forces were routed, and the General taken prisoner and confined to one of the log huts serving as a guardhouse. He escaped and rejoined the fight, throwing snowballs gleefully, when he

was informed that he had not been paroled. Some threatened joking-
ly to dunk the general in the icy waters of Mill Creek for this infringe-
ment of the rules. He pleaded that he would not do it again and to
forgive him, for it was a first time offense. Good-naturedly, the victors
relented.[11]

Patrick and Susan's wedding plans had to be put on hold that
spring, when the war came sweeping back into their lives with a force
that even love could not conquer. The April weather smelled of a
mountain Spring in bloom, and Cleburne drilled his troops, had rifle
and artillery practice and often sham battles using blanks. At Dalton
on May 3, Maj. Gen. Joseph E. Johnston, newly appointed commander of the Army of Tennessee, began massing and assembling
his army. At the highest effective count, he had 75,000 men. Coming
down from the North on his invasion of Georgia was Maj. Gen.
William T. Sherman with at least 100,000.

Johnston sent his best division to meet the enemy. It was that
of Pat Cleburne. Always personally overseeing the deployment of his
command, his first encounter with Sherman's troops was at Rocky
Face Ridge. Here began the waltz that would end four months later
at Jonesboro, Georgia. The Atlanta Campaign had begun. Every
inch of Sherman's advance was stubbornly contested by Johnston's
fortifications, and every heavily entrenched Confederate position was
outflanked and sidestepped by Sherman's elusive movements, away
from Johnston and toward Atlanta.

Pat Cleburne was considered by many to be the best general
Johnston had at his command. His division won for itself a war
record of glory. The battles mounted through the spring months—
Snake Creek Gap, Resaca, Adairsville, Cassville, Allatoona Pass.
Pickett's Mill on May 27 was an astounding Confederate victory—
solely attributed to Pat Cleburne's skillful handling of his forces. It
was called "Pat Cleburne's great fight" by his veterans. There is no
doubt his sweetheart in Mobile was proud of her general.[12]

From here the Union forces shifted to Kennesaw Mountain,
another great victory for the South. Now war separated the lovers,
each fighting it in their own way. While Pat was engaged in a daily
struggle to halt giving ground, with Atlanta at his back, Sue was

threatened by the Union fleet in Mobile Bay. The family was faced with the realization that they may have to become refugees, and flee deep into Alabama. If she left Mobile, Sue would lose contact with any letters from Pat. However, the mail was still getting through to Atlanta, and for now the forts in the outer islands of the Bay were holding firm.[13]

After Kennesaw, a change occurred which rocked the Army to its core. Gen. Joe Johnston was relieved of command. The new general was John Bell Hood, freshly arrived from Lee's Army of Northern Virginia—and his decisions would have grave consequences for thousands of soldiers in the Army of Tennessee. Fate had set in motion a clockwork for disaster—and Pat Cleburne and Sue Tarleton would be caught up in it.

The strategy of the army drastically changed. Hood went from the defensive to the offensive in two attacks that lost Atlanta. Peachtree Creek and the Battle of Atlanta, fought July 21 through 23, were devastating in their death tolls. Over 5,000 Southern boys were killed. Pat Cleburne's men had been responsible for capturing the part of the Union works that had been taken. It is reflected in his casualty reports. He had lost 1,388 men, more than half his strength engaged.[14]

Away from this center of war, Susan and her sister Grace were on a visit to Mary Hardee in LaGrange, Georgia. No doubt Susan hoped that perhaps Patrick may have a short leave and meet her there, but it was impossible. She and Grace visited relatives in Tuskegee and returned to Mobile in July.

Bloodied and spent, the Army of Tennessee pulled back, awaiting orders from Hood. A siege set in for 28 days while they waited for Sherman's next move.

In Mobile, Sue Tarleton had prayed, fretted, and eagerly watched the newspapers for three months—dreading what she may hear. Every letter that arrived in Pat's handwriting was the answer to a prayer, as she lived a nervous, day to day existence. Mobile was being threatened by the Union fleet under Admiral David Farragut, and her brother Robert was at Fort Morgan, part of the outer defenses of Mobile Bay. Fort Morgan fell in the Battle of Mobile on August 23, after a two week siege, and Robert was taken prisoner.

Though her brother was in danger as well, it was different with Pat. He was a general, who insisted on being at the head of his men. Had she complained and pleaded that he stay in the rear, he would only have quoted to her his family crest. It reads "Forward! The Cleburnes cannot do otherwise." He had lived up to that motto with pride. It was the reason his men loved him.[15]

Sue continued to write twice a week, agonizing over every word in answer to the long epistles he sent her. One was seventeen pages long! She wrote a rough draft, carefully composing her replies, before copying the finished letter neatly on her stationary. The rough drafts, she bundled together, and kept them locked in her writing desk like precious cargo. Patrick wrote as often as the fighting would allow. His aide and close friend Lt. Leonard H.Mangum recalled his commander sharing his feelings and love for Sue in this touching account:

> "Letters which he wrote to his betrothed were some-
> times read...amid some quiet camp scenes, and were
> often revelations, even to one who knew him well, as
> to the depth of his feelings. Devoid of all approach to
> sentimentality, they were full of a most sweet and ten-
> der passion. They detailed the author's thoughts and
> fancies in a style that was both elevated and beautiful,
> and in every line they were glowing with an affection
> that was exquisite in its pathos and tenderness."[16]

The siege of Atlanta ended on September 8, after the battle of Jonesboro. Sherman struck out toward Macon, while Hood contemplated what to do. He decided not to pursue his enemy for the time being, and a short lull occurred in the fighting.

Cleburne's thoughts now turned to Sue. He had not seen her for months. He wrote that he would apply for leave beginning sometime around the first of October. Then perhaps they could get married. It would only be a little longer.

When he put in his request for a furlough, Pat Cleburne was told that it was impossible. The Army of Tennessee was opening its

fall campaign commencing on September 29, with a march into
Tennessee, to attack the Union army at Nashville, and draw
Sherman out of Georgia and onto Hood's chosen ground. He broke
the disappointing news to Susan, who reiterated her feelings to Sallie
Lightfoot:

> "I received a letter from the Genl. which put an end
> to my writing for the day, and sent me off for a good
> cry. You must know he had been counting on a fur-
> lough for some time and expected to get it about the
> first of this month. Well! on the 28th when he went to
> apply, Hood informed him that the next day his
> Corps was to move across the Chattahoochee and
> take such a position in Sherman's rear as would break
> up his communications. This puts an end to his visit,
> and what grieves me more, is but the commencement
> of another long and arduous campaign. I don't know
> how I am going to get through it, the past one has
> nearly used me up; everyone is telling me how thin
> and badly I am looking. I believe I have had a regu-
> lar fit of "the blues".[17]

The Army of Tennessee marched North, and on the evening
of November 29, camped at Spring Hill, Tennessee, in preparation
for an assualt on the Union Army.

Patrick Cleburne, in the prime of his life, had everything to
live for, as he stood before Gen. John Bell Hood on the last day of
November outside the picturesque little farming community of
Franklin, Tennessee. Federal forces had occupied it and built three
formidable rings of breastworks around its center. The order from
Hood—take those breastworks.

What he demanded would be a disaster. Pat was distraught
after hearing the decision. It was as if he had a premonition of all he
feared coming true, but was helpless to prevent it. He was not the
commander in chief. His officers and aides, those closest to Cleburne,
noticed a despondency in him like never before.[18]

But he was not one to flinch from duty. "If we are to die, let us die like men" he told one of his brigadiers. Cleburne's Division spearheaded the charge on Franklin. They took the first ring of works, easily driving the enemy into the next.Pat had two horses shot from under him. Finally dismounted, he put his kepi on his sword, drew his pistol and went into the charge with his men, yelling encouragement and urging his veterans on. The men got to the second line of defenses, and taking it, halted in the ditches, panting and waiting for their beloved general to tell them what to do next. They anticipated it would be to attack, and steeled themselves for the orders as darkness fell.[19]

"We waited and waited and waited," recalled one soldier. "And the boys kept crying for the word and wondered why it didn't come. But when it didn't come, I knew Pat Cleburne was dead, for if he had been living he would have given us that order."[20]

Franklin was a Confederate victory, but with a hollow ring. At dawn, Cleburne's men began searching for him, hoping he had only been wounded or captured. But they found him, lying 50 yards from the Union works, where he had been left by a burial detail. He lay on his back, a peaceful look on his face, his cap partly over his eyes. The new gray coat he had donned before the battle was unbuttoned and open, revealing the large bloodstain beneath his heart, a brilliant crimson against his white linen shirt.[21]

As word spread that Cleburne was killed, his men wept openly, and inconsolably. His body was taken to the nearby home of Mr. John W. McGavock, where he lay on the veranda of the spacious mansion, one of six generals to die that day—more than in any battle of any war.Later he was removed to the home of William Julius Polk outside Columbia. Here, the general's body was washed, dressed "in plain clothes", and laid out in the family parlor before being placed in a walnut coffin made by a local cabinet maker. His aide, Leonard Mangum, found among the general's things the handkerchief given to him by Sue. He placed it over the General's face. Her beloved Pat was buried at St. John's Churchyard on December 2, a quaint old cemetery like the ones back home in "the Old Country".[22]

Sue Tarleton had heard nothing from Tennessee. It was December 5, a stark, raw winter day. Even the newspaper had been behind with the latest reports from Hood's Army. Most news was at least a week old. She went out into the garden to walk and think. Where she and Pat had sat amid the budding spring was now stark and bare, its beauty dormant beneath its winter undress. As she looked across the street, a newsboy stood on the corner. Passersby were stopping and gaping at the headlines of his paper, as he cried out. Curious at what could be inducing people to act so, she ventured closer. "Reports from Tennessee!" he cried. "Victory Near Franklin"- "Cleburne and other Generals Killed!"[23]

Killed! The word pierced her heart like an arrow. Stunned by the horrible scene her mind grappled to accept, she stared, speechless. A sick feeling overcame her before she collapsed in a faint.

The shock and grief sent her to bed for several days, unable to face the reality she had so often forced out of her thoughts. For months she had dreaded each campaign, held her breath at the news of each battle. He had always come through unscathed, to reassure her of their future together. Now he would never come again. Her future lay cold and still in the Tennessee hills, snatched from her life as suddenly as he had come into it. Never again would she hear that Irish voice whisper loving words in her ear, feel his protective embrace, or look into those kind, expressive eyes that commanded such character and strength. Broken-hearted, deprived of saying good-bye at his funeral, or visiting a grave, which would have been some kind of comfort to one left behind, she exchanged her wedding gown for the black dress of mourning.[24]

Patrick Cleburne had requested that in the event of his death, all personal belongings be sent to his friend of many years, Dr. Charles Nash. He would know what to do.

Before Christmas, a box arrived for Sue Tarleton. In it were some of Pat's things—among them a beautiful presentation sword and swordbelt, one of his cherished possessions, given to him by his regiment, the 15th Arkansas. Folded along with this, was a flag—one his division had captured at Ringgold Gap a year earlier. It had been wrested from troops of the 29th Missouri Volunteer Infantry in the fight, and held great significance to his men. They wanted her to have it. She cherished these relics for the rest of her life.[25]

The winter of 1864-65 saw the Confederacy losing ground. When Hood's defeated army arrived back in Alabama, some were sent to Mobile to strengthen the defenses there. But by March 1865, the city was in a state of siege. All civilians were urged to leave, taking property and servants into the interior. The Union bombardment of the city was often intense. The two hour firing on April 4, was so heavy that citizens could feel the vibrations and hear the reports of the heavy siege guns across the bay. Spanish Fort, the last Confederate outer work, fell on April 8, 1865. Soldiers retreating through Mobile alarmed citizens. Cotton was gathered for burning, to prevent it from falling into the hands of the Yankees. The Tarleton warehouses were emptied and added to the pile.[26]

It mattered little to Sue. The light had gone out of her life, and darkness fell like a heavy curtain on her very existence and spirit. The Union occupation which commenced on the afternoon of April 12 was just another affront. She could have endured it as long as there was something to endure it for, while her champion was fighting. But her champion was dead, and there was nothing in the foreseeable future but oppression and hard times. She merely existed, hiding herself away in her mourning from the vulgar eyes of her oppressors. When Union soldiers sought entertainment and hospitality among the citizens of Mobile, the Tarleton door was shut in their face.[27]

After the war, a young man came to Mobile seeking a new start. He looked up his old classmate from Princeton, Robert Tarleton, hoping his friendship could be renewed and lead to a job position. He had corresponded with Robert in July 1864, when Robert invited him to his wedding.

Hugh L. Cole had fought in the late war as Captain Cole of a company in the 2nd North Carolina Infantry. He also served as enrolling officer in the Confederate service. Leaving his native state and hometown in New Bern, North Carolina to find a law profession, amid Reconstruction and Yankee occupation, he did not know what to expect from Mobile, but decided to take his chances.[28]

Robert Tarleton was glad to see his old friend. After reminiscing on their Princeton days, and exchanging war stories, Hugh was introduced to Robert and Sallie's infant son, and Robert's sister, Sue Tarleton. Though officially past the mourning period, and the trappings of black crepe, her heart was still filled with grief.

As the months went by, and with Robert's coaxing, Sue was convinced that her life must go on. Hugh found her attractive, and a courtship began. She once again accepted a man's proposal of marriage, and became Mrs. Hugh L. Cole on October 9, 1867.[29]

The following summer found the young couple expecting their first child. They were living at Point Clear, away from the city heat in Mobile. It was a gathering place for the wealthy, a community of summerhouses near the bay. Suddenly, on June 30, Sue suffered a cerebral hemorrhage. Hugh, frantic and unable to find a doctor, ran along the beach in search of help. But there was none to be found. Susan Tarleton Cole died almost immediately.[30]

Robert Tarleton, never having recovered his health from his prison experience, died of a severe infection of the vital organs on September 28, 1868. Hugh Cole had no reason for remaining in Mobile. The Reconstruction policies forbade him to practice his law profession, further driving him to seek a change. "I need not tell you that I am utterly cast down," he wrote to another former schoolmate on October 10. "I am most sincerely trying to submit to the will of our Father in Heaven, but my troubles come so thick and fast that it is hard to do...This has been a long, sorrowful letter. Indeed everything in this once happy section seems black as Egyptian darkness." He left this tragic scene in 1869, for New York, where he remarried and found a position with the firm of Davis, Cole and Rapallo in New York City. He died November 5, 1898 at Southampton, New York.[31]

Sue Tarleton's story ends at her grave in Magnolia Cemetery. Her headstone reads:

"A little while, and she was animate;
A little while, and she is Death's pale bride;
A little while, and holy, sanctified,
She stands before God's throne immaculate."

In 1870, Pat Cleburne's remains were moved to his adopted hometown of Helena, Arkansas. He was buried on a knoll overlooking the river, near the woods where he used to stroll as a young man. They lie far apart, two lives who briefly lived and loved and touched one another, whose story is but a fleeting moment in the great march of time, but whose untimely deaths leave us to ponder what might have been.

Maj. Gen. Patrick Cleburne
(Courtesy Alabama Dept. of Archives and History)

Susan Tarleton
(Courtesy Mrs. Bedford Moore)

Capt. Robert Tarleton
(Courtesy Mrs. Bedford Moore)

Capt. Hugh Cole
(Courtesy Princeton University)

Notes

[1] Howell and Elizabeth Purdue. *Pat Cleburne, Confederate General,* (Hillsboro, TX: Hill Jr. College Press, 1973), 284-285.

[2] Ibid., 286.

[3] Tarleton Family Collection. Yale University. Robert Tarleton and Sarah B. Lightfoot were married November 22, 1864. Grace Tarleton and Henry Goldthwaite married February. 3, 1864. Marriage records of Montgomery County.

[4] Charles L. Dufour. *Nine Men in Gray* (Garden City, NY: Doubleday and Co.,1963), 104.

[5] Dufour, 83; John Francis MaGuire, M.P. *The Irish in America* (London: Longman's, Green, and Co., 1868), 653.

[6] Purdue, 287.

[7] Buck Family Papers. Southern Historical Collection, University of North Carolina. Irving Buck to his sister, February 9, 1864.

[8] Cleburne to Sallie Lightfoot, March 11, 1864. Tarleton Family Papers.

[9] Ibid.

[10] Purdue, 295.

[11] Ibid., 296.

[12] Ibid., 322.

[13] Arthur W. Bergeron, Jr. *Confederate Mobile.* (Jackson, MS: University Press of Mississippi, 1991), 140-151.

[14] U.S. War Department. War of the Rebellion: Official Records of the Union and Confederate Armies. Vol. 38, pt. 3, 733, 741, 748. U.S. Government Printing Office, Washington, D.C. 1880-1901.

[15] Bergeron, 149-150; Robert Tarleton served in Co. A, 3rd Ala. Inf. before becoming a second lieutenant in Co. E, 1st Battalion Alabama

Artillery, Smith's Battery. Compiled Service Records of Soldiers in Alabama Regiments; Purdue, 2.

[16] Purdue, 339.

[17] Tarleton Family Papers.

[18] Dufour,114-115.

[19] Ibid., 117.

[20] Purdue, 430.

[21] Dufour, 117-118; Purdue, 431-32.

[22] Purdue, 432.

[23] Ray Charles Curtis, "The Homecoming of Pat Cleburne", *Southern Partisan* Magazine. Summer Issue, 1984, 40.

[24] Purdue, 433.

[25] Dr. Charles Edward Nash. *Biographical Sketches of Gen. Pat Cleburne and Gen. T.C. Hindman.* Reprint, (Dayton, OH: Morningside Press, 1977), 111-114. The sword is on display at the Atlanta History Center.

[26] Bergeron, 188-192; Conversation between author and Mrs. Bedford Moore.

[27] Information provided by Mrs. Bedford Moore.

[28] Obituary of Hugh L. Cole. *New York Times*, November 6, 1898.

[29] Tarleton Family Papers.

[30] Death Records of Mobile County.

[31] November 6, 1898. Letter from Hugh L. Cole to —Kellogg, Oct. 10, 1868. Cole file at Princeton University. Death Certificate of Robert Tarleton.

6

THE NURSE:
ELLA K. NEWSOM TRADER
"The Florence Nightingale of the Southern Army"

By
Barbara Duffey

Ella K. Newsom Trader began her life as the eldest daughter of Rev. T. S. N. King, a Baptist minister of Brandon, Mississippi. At an early age she learned by her father's example that one's purpose in life was to make personal sacrifices by ministering to the sick and suffering of this world.

In a letter she reports:

> "I was born in the little town of Brandon, Mississippi. The village looked like a big ant hill and the population though small was just about as thriving and active as the busy ant. My father was a Baptist minister and pastor of the only church of that peculiar people in the town. He was quite well off in this world's goods and my mother coming of an aristocratic family chose to hold herself rather aloof from the church. We always had a carriage with two red bays and a buggy with a big brown horse. The first thing I remember of my childhood is that Pump ran away one morning as mother and we children got into the buggy to go to Sunday school and all of us were tumbled out in a heap."[1]

When Ella was still a young girl, Reverend King moved his family to the wilds of Arkansas where Ella soon became an accomplished horsewoman. The adversities of pioneering life helped prepare Ella for the difficult sacrifices she would endure during the War Between the States.

When Ella matured into a young woman she fell in love with Dr. Frank Newsom, a highly accomplished physician of that region, and they were soon married. But shortly after their marriage he was taken ill and died, cruelly severing their deep bond of love and leaving her a helpless, grieving widow of twenty two. But fortunately she was amply taken care of by his vast wealth and land investments.

Out of Ella's richly endowed religious nature and the deep sorrow only felt by a tender young widow emerged a strength and resolve that Ella Newsom carried with her as she unselfishly ministered to the wounded and suffering soldiers of the newly formed Confederacy. [2]

In the spring of 1861 from Ella's country home, 160 acres on Sand Mountain, she prepared for the imminent war. Sand Mountain is located at the pinacle corner of three states, Alabama, Georgia and Tennessee. On top of that mountain the Gordons, Guilfords of Boston, Dr. La Compt of Georgia, a Mr. Grant, brother of L.P. Grant, who gave to Atlanta "Grant Park," and Ella Newsom had homes. Together they owned nearly all of the mountain and intended to create out of it an area much like the famous Blannerhassett Island of Aaron Burr's fame. But their dreams vanished with the talk of war.[3]

She and her friends set about making clothes for the troops and much needed blankets. Unable to supply the demand for blankets, the Gordons and Mrs. Newsom created their own invention to serve the need. They pasted together large sheets of heavy paper the size of a blanket and covered each side with calico. This made a protection from the damp ground and a light burden when rolled up. [4]

In the autumn of 1861, driven by her desire to pursue hospital work, Mrs. Newsom visited Memphis, Tennessee, and began her instruction in nursing at the city Hospital under the charge of Dr. James Keller and the Roman Catholic Sisters. Later she worked in the Southern Mother's Home in the charge of Mrs. Sarah Gordon Law.

After the battle of Belmont, Missouri on November 6, 1861, between the Union forces under Maj. Gen. U. S. Grant and the Confederates under Gen. Leonidas "Bishop" Polk at Columbus, Kentucky, the need for nurses rose dramatically. Mrs. Newsom worked for a time with the Overton Hospital at Memphis where the sick and wounded were nursed and because of her expertise she soon became its director.[5]

Mrs. Newsom's experiences were identified mainly with the Army of Tennessee, in the hospitals of Bowling Green, Nashville, Memphis, Chattanooga, Corinth, Marietta, Atlanta and other points.[6]

On August 21, 1861, the Confederate Congress authorized the employment of 'nurses and cooks' under those subject to military control and in no case to receive pay above that allowed to enlisted men or volunteers." The hiring of attendants white or black didn't improve the quality of the nursing care. Many of the slaves in the hospitals were hired by the year and the Medical Director William A. Carrington said, "Negro wenches were one of the greatest pests and nuisances about a hospital." [7]

In the early months of the war in 1861, the Confederacy's medical department was unorganized, without a head or a hospital. On September 18, 1861, Col. Samuel H. Stout set up the first Confederate hospital in Bowling Green, Kentucky, that was soon to become a model for others. He "used Mr. W. B. Patilloe's house" as a hospital at the rate of fourteen dollars per month for the Third Tennessee Regiment. With winter setting in,the shelter of a house would provide more protection for his wounded soldiers. Most of the hospital facilities at that time were merely tents erected for the duration needed, then dismantled and moved to the next battle site.[8]

That same day Confederate Gen. Simon Bolivar Buckner occupied Bowling Green with his 4,500 troops. In October the Arkansas and Tennessee infantry and cavalry numbered nearly 10,000 men. The conflicts began on December 17, 1861, at Rowlett's Station where hundreds of men were killed or wounded.[9]

Soon the wounded arrived at Bowling Green in massive numbers, from the first skirmishes in Missouri and on the Kentucky border, quickly outnumbering beds. When at all possible, private homes, hotels, and public buildings were all commandeered as hospitals. The nursing care was primitive and unorganized in every way and mostly delivered by male volunteers or the walking injured who had never nursed before. One patient claimed that he had "miserable nurses" who did not "know Castor Oil from a gun rod nor laudanum from a hole in the ground."[10]

Women nurses were frowned upon early in the war because it was thought that nursing young male soldiers might compromise the delicate and modest natures of young women. The Confederate Congress passed an "act to better provide for the sick and wounded of the army in hospitals," in September of 1861. This law provided allotment to each hospital for two matrons, two assistant matrons, two matrons for each ward and such other cooks and nurses as might be needed and the supply of their room and rations. After that time the Southern army welcomed women as nurses.[11]

According to Fraise Richard in his book on Ella:

"In December of 1861, Mrs. Newsom took her own servants and a boxcar load of supplies, at her own expense, and rushed to Bowling Green to alleviate in her estimation the almost inexpressible sufferings of the confederate sick. The scenes of destitution among the troops were of beggar description. Want of organization, lack of suitable buildings, scarcity of supplies and the exceedingly cold weather caused untold suffering. With tireless energy she consecrated her energies to this distressing condition, often laboring from 4 o'clock in the morning until 12 o'clock at night."[12]

When Gen. J. B. Floyd's troops arrived in Bowling Green his surgeon-in-chief was so impressed with Mrs. Newsom's work that he gave her full charge of all the hospitals in Bowling Green. After Forts Donaldson and Henry surrendered, she moved to Nashville and organized the Howard High School into a hospital for the sick and wounded of those forts.

As the Confederates withdrew from Nashville, Mrs. Newsom performed some remarkable feats, to hasten a quick retreat:

"With the aid of Col. Dunn she had the sick and wounded placed upon boxcars and taken to Winchester, Tenn. After several days' wearisome movements, the train reached Deckerd. The engineer, for some reason, detached the engine leaving the long train with its helpless passengers standing dark and unprotected on the track at 10 o'clock at night. Wandering about the engine yard, Mrs. Newsom secured another engine and by 2 o'clock had her train safely lodged at Winchester, distant several miles. All the churches and schools of the place were converted into hospitals and every arrangement made for the comfort of the unfortunate men, who were so pleased with the treatment that they called the place "Soldiers' Paradise."

Mrs. Newsom's stay at Winchester was also brief. The Confederate Army concentrated at Corinth for the desperate battle of Shiloh under the leadership of Gen. Albert Sidney Johnston, April 6th and 7th, 1862. On leave in Atlanta, Mrs. Newsom received an urgent request from Maj. Gen. Pat Cleburne to come immediately to Corinth and bring with her a carload of supplies. She complied immediately, taking with her Carrie, her trusted servant.[13]

The battle of Shiloh proved to be the most ghastly bloodbath in the History of the Western Hemisphere to that date: with more than 1,700 men killed, and 8,000 wounded on each side, a total of 16,500 wounded from both armies.[14]

The wounded from Shiloh were brought to Corinth and required all the nurses that could be summoned from the Southwestern States. Bandages were furnished by the women of the South and fashioned out of sheets, spreads, skirts and other worn out goods. Old linen was scraped with a knife to make lint and a good substitute for the latter was raw cotton baked in an oven until it was charred. Sponges became scarce and clean linen or cotton rags were used instead.[15]

Mrs. Newsom speaking of these scenes said:

"The scenes in the Tishamingo Hotel Hospital after the battle of Shiloh beggar all description. Every yard of space on the floors, as well as all the beds, bunks and cots were covered with the mangled forms of dying and dead soldiers. All had come from the battlefield several miles distant, many having been conveyed in rough wagons over muddy roads. When they arrived at any of the hospital buildings the first thing one of the women attendants had to do was to get some coffee and bread to revive the body a little so that the wounds could be dressed as soon as possible. Next was to find a hospital suit in order to rid them of the muddy and bloody clothes in which they had fallen. In the midst of the confusion of the day in question a bevy of women from Mobile, Alabama, under the supervision of an Episcopal minister arrived. They styled themselves the 'Florence Nightingale Brigade.' Immediately after their arrival they held a council of criticism and decided to revolutionize the bad management. In less than a week, however, only two or three of thirty were left to give a helping hand. One was Miss Cumming of Mobile, Alabama, a Scotch lady and a Mrs. Crocker. All took hold of the work heart and soul, and remained in the Hospital service to the end of the war, Miss Cumming afterwards writing a book, 'Hospital Life in the Confederacy,' and a few years later bringing out another book, 'Gleanings from the Southland.'

I left the Tishomingo Hotel in charge of Mrs. Gilmore and Miss Cumming and took the Corinth House Hospital were there was not a corner in which a woman could lay her head for rest or sleep. I was forced to go to the private residence of a Mr. Inge which was at that time the Army headquarters. I was allowed to occupy with my faithful servant Carrie a small room in which we put cots and one or two boxes for seats. Every morning at daylight we went to the Hospital remaining there until eleven or twelve every night that we didn't sit up with some poor fellow shot in the lungs and who had to be fanned every moment to enable him to breathe at all.

Among this number I remember a soldier from the enemy's ranks who was a prisoner with many others. He was a splendid looking man with great big brown eyes. His name was never given to me. I shall never forget the agony of that suffering countenance as he tossed his head from side to side to try to breathe. When he learned that we were about to leave on a retreat, he begged so hard to be taken along that I persuaded some of the nurses and soldiers to take up his bunk and carry it to the car platform and if it were possible I promised him he should be put on the train with our wounded. Carrie, my maid, walked beside the bunk fanning him every step of the way; yet we pleaded but vainly to have him go with our wounded. The Yankees were then shelling the town and I had to tell him that his friends would soon take charge of him and see that he was well cared for.Carrie and I bade him farewell at the same time placing a fan in his hand; then we boarded the train—I never heard of or saw him again.[16]

Kate Cumming remarked in her diary about meeting Mrs. Newsom at Corinth:

May 26. This morning I visited Mrs. Williamson and Mrs. Crocker who came from Mobile with us. They are in a hospital at the Corinth House. I saw a Mrs. Newsom. I do not recollect that I was ever more struck with a face at first sight than hers. It expressed more purity and goodness than I had ever seen before. I asked Mrs. Williamson who she was. She informed me that she was a rich widow from Arkansas and had surrendered all the comforts of home to do what she could for the suffering of our army. She had been with it since the commencement of the war and had spent a great deal of money. Mrs. Williamson also informed me that her face did not belie the goodness and purity of her heart; and that she was a Christian in the purest sense of the word. I hope that we have many such among us. I cannot imagine why it is that I have heard so little about her." [17]

After her experience at Corinth, Mrs. Newsom took a short leave to visit a close friend, Miss Augusta Evans. While on her brief stay she inspected the hospitals at Okolona, Columbus and Meridian, Mississippi.

General Floyd had asked her to come to Western Virginia and oversee the care of his wounded soldiers. This she did in the summer of 1862 when she went to Abingdon, the seat of Emory and Henry College which had been turned into a hospital under the direction of Dr. Forbes.

While at this place she decided to go to Richmond to increase her knowledge in medical matters. Her trip coincided with the battle of Seven Pines on May 31 and June 1, 1862. The heavy losses on each side equaled to 7,000 out of 15,000 men killed and wounded. Her stay was brief because she became ill and returned to her mountain retreat in Buchanan, where she wrote a very spiritual letter to Gen. Preston Smith:[18]

Buchanan, August 24, 1862.

General Preston Smith
My Kind Friend:—

I sat in the door and watched the daylight depart; the eyelids of evening close; the soft and gentle breeze of these mountain homes fanned my face and stole quietly away, and now the outer world slumbers on the couch of night....

It is a Sabbath night too and may I not so earnestly pray and desire that all my correspondence and conversation with gentlemen would elevate and enable their thoughts and aspirations...?

I was wondering this evening if you have contemplated scenes beyond the grave, and seriously considered the question whether you were ready for an exchange of worlds. Perhaps you may think my Sabbath evening thoughts too serious for correspondence but they originated from what you wrote me of the grand and gorgeous sunset you and your brother had gazed upon and enjoyed so much. I wonder if while feasting your eye on so magnificent a scene of creation, your soul were not subdued and your spirit unconsciously bowed in adoration of its creator....

Are you not astonished at yourself that you should have lived so long the abject worshiper of your own evil nature? Sometime we must adore and worship; and if it be not the supreme ruler of the Universe it must be some God of our own make.

Sometimes when I find myself communing with absent friends, I feel such a bursting and longing of soul for them to yield their sinful nature to the regenerating influence of the Holy Spirit that I feel surely they must, they will soon acknowledge God as the supreme object of all worship. But the power to convince and to convert men from the errors of their ways belongs alone to God and O what a feeble instrument I am to endeavor to persuade them that in religion alone is fullness of joy....

I feel so disappointed to learn that you have left Knoxville; for I thought brother could visit me. He was near and I could hear from home. Still I am glad that you are pushing on to drive the foul invader from downtrodden Kentucky. We ought to have had the go-ahead movement long ago. Do not get too far off without writing.

You must be tired of this long letter, I will close, Good by.

Your Friend,
E. K. Newsom

After being called to Chattanooga, Mrs. Newsom became matron of a hospital in the Crutchfield House in October of 1862, where with her servants she worked as heroically as ever.[19] This building was used as a receiving hospital since it was located near the train station. A guard stood outside to check the passes of all who entered.[20]

Kate Cumming speaks of the "Newsom Hospital" in Chattanooga, named in honor of Ella Newsom before her arrival in that city:

> Sept. 4, 1862: Chattanooga . . . . In the afternoon we paid a visit to another hospital in town where Mrs. May met an old friend in the surgeon, Dr Hunter. He was glad to see her and asked her to come into his hospital. He was going to have it enlarged and would like to have Mrs. Williamson and myself, besides Mrs. May, but as Dr. Stout, the post surgeon, did not approve of more than one lady in a hospital, he could not take us without asking him. He took us all through his hospital. It was the upper part of a long row of warehouses with windows East and West. The partitions between were taken away making large wards where a current of air could blow right through. There were some four or five of these rooms opening into each other. The whole was well white-washed. I thought the smell of lime better than disinfectant of all the camphor or cologne in the world. The name of this hospital is the "Newsom;" so called in honor of the lady I met and admired in Corinth.[21]

Kate Cumming's diary continues:

> *November 9*: Had a visit a few evenings ago from Mrs. Newsom. She has charge of a new hospital that is opened in the Crutchfield House called the "Foard," in honor of the medical director of this army. [22]

November 11: I went out shopping with Mrs. Newsom and was quite amused at a bargain she was trying to make with a woman who had potatoes to sell. She tried to get them on credit; but the woman was inexorable and would not give them, even with all the tales that Mrs. Newsom told of the sick men needing them. The woman said she had no faith in hospitals paying; so Mrs. Newsom had to come away without them and wait until she got the money. She is expecting some soon—the proceeds of a concert given by the ladies of the place.[23]

November 16: I called on Mrs. Newsom this morning and found her cooking dinner for about fifty men on a small grate; she had to cook one article at a time.Mrs. Newsom was in distress on account of news she had just received from her home in Arkansas. We went on a foraging expedition in search of milk and found a woman who would sell us a quantity of buttermilk—a treat for the patients. We went round by the river part of the road. It was the wildest scenery I ever beheld.In one moment we were in a ravine so deep as almost to exclude from view the blue of heaven (a nice haunt for boggles and witches). At another time I trembled lest my horse might stumble and cast me into the ravine below. Mrs. Newsom rode on as fearlessly as any knight of old or one of our own cavalry. I believe the latter are the best horsemen in the world, the Indians not excepted.[24]

January 16: I have just returned from another horseback ride with Mrs. Newsom; we visited a small-pox hospital, but were not allowed to go in; about six of Mrs. Newsom's nurses were there as patients. She inquired how they were and if they needed anything. They have very nice quarters, one of our ablest surgeons—Dr. Kratz—to attend them. The mortality from this loathsome disease is little or nothing. (It

must have been the mild form.) As I rode along side
of this angelic woman and listened to her conversation, I discovered a combination of admirable traits
in her character, such as I'd never met in any woman
before...[25]

After coming to her post in the Crutchfield House, Mrs.
Newsom was assigned as chief matron of the Academy Hospital, in
which she served until debility caused by long and laborious services
forced her to seek rest.[26]

The Academy Hospital occupied the Masonic Academy
building on College Hill in Chattanooga, Tennessee.Dr. Hawkins,
who was to become one of the most famous surgeons of the South,
was the Academy surgeon. The facility had wards one-story high,
each holding about twenty-five patients. For every two wards there
was a small distributing room. The food was brought from the
kitchen to these rooms and distributed by a ward matron. Mrs.
Newsom directed that the wards be whitewashed and decorated with
evergreens. The hospital attendants stayed in tents some of which
had carpet and chimneys. A wash house, a linen room, ironing room
and a shed for drying the clothes in wet weather were available at the
Academy. [27]

Gen. Braxton B. Bragg and several of his respected surgeons
including Dr. A.J. Foard paid a surprise visit to the Academy and
Newsom hospitals, inspecting them for proper medical care. The
next morning Dr. Foard informed Dr. Stout that General Bragg was
highly pleased with his findings, claiming that these were the only
hospitals fit to treat soldiers that he'd seen.[28]

Several days later Dr. Stout received word that he had been
named superintendent of all the general hospitals of the army and of
the department commanded by Bragg. Part of his job was to locate and
assign officers to these institutions and improve facilities as needed.[29]

On Academy Hill Dr. Stout had built specially designed
structures intended to provide well ventilated wards known as
"pavillion hospitals." These became the standard type of military
hospital building used for years. They were operated by the Gilmer

and the Academy Hospitals and cared for the majority of battle wounded.[30]

Kate Cummings recorded in her diary:

March 16: "There are now four hospitals in this place: the Academy, of which Dr. Hawthorn is the chief surgeon and Mrs. Newsom matron; the Foard, of which Mrs. Crocker of Mobile is matron…and our own, the Newsom. We found Mrs. Newsom for a wonder at leisure, her hospital is a very fine one; it is on a very top of a hill, commanding a view of the whole town. After I left her we went in search of milk.[31]

Union "Colonel" Ned Wentworth, a Western officer, possibly from Michigan or Illinois, was injured at Stone's River and taken as a prisoner to Chattanooga where he was placed in a hospital under the direction of Mrs. Newsom. When she found him severely wounded and asked his condition, he said, "Oh, Mrs. Newsom. you wouldn't be so kind if you knew who I am; I am on the enemy's side."

"But," she said. "you are fallen and I make no distinction."

They became good friends. He lived eight months in a tent devoted to gangrene patients. His arm was amputated in August, he died from the effects a few days later.

Wentworth was said to be a relative of "Long" John Wentworth, of Chicago, subsequently a member of Congress from that city.[32]

The battle of Chickamauga was fought September 19-20, after Bragg moved his army into North Georgia, resulting in the retreat of the Union army and the besieging of it within the confines of Chattanooga. But the battle cost the Confederates 18,454 casualties, nearly thirty percent of their force.[33] The Confederate hospitals were moved out of town to locations a safe distance further south to Rome, Marietta and other points.

As a result of the heavy 1863 engagements, Mrs. Newsom was empowered to take possession of and organize hospitals in substantially all the buildings around the Public Square in Marietta.

They were held by her for more than a year—until Confederate Gen. Joseph E. Johnston's retreat in 1864 rendered the possession of Marietta by the Confederates impossible.[34]

Ella spent the winter of 1863-64 in Cobb County:

> Hardly had the guns stilled at Chickamauga when hospital trains began to roll South, straw-littered boxcars with hungry wounded, whose undressed injuries were tortured by the rough ride. Detrained at Marietta, they were placed in improvised hospitals in the Courthouse, in stores around the Park Square, in churches and in the Georgia Military Institute buildings. Marietta women rallied to the need; they prepared broth and other special foods, helped dose and dress wounds; wrote letters to loved ones, and in general made life bearable to these men who had undergone so much. These hospitals operated almost until the fall of Marietta the next summer when patients and staff were moved further South—the sites then became Federal hospitals upon Northern occupation. [35]

Chattanooga's Academy Hospital transferred to Marietta, Georgia and later moved on to Atlanta, Forsyth, Auburn, Alabama, Corinth, Mississippi and back to Auburn.[36]

Mrs. Newsom remained with the hospital in Marietta and then at Atlanta, moving with it until the end of the war.[37] She gives us insight into her personal relationships with familiar names associated with the Confederate Army, in her post-war account:

> I had resolved to lay all I possessed of youth, beauty and wealth on the altar of the Confederacy. So of course I did not expect to be known outside of the hospitals. But I soon found that I must be thrown with officers of the highest rank to secure what I needed in keeping a suffering army, bunks and pallets in even a moderately comfortable condition. So it was, I suppose, because of my

youthful appearance and my enthusiastic ardor in the hospital work, I became quite a favorite with our Generals, all of whom were humane enough to want their men as well cared for in sickness or when wounded as conditions would allow. I had a personal acquaintance with many of them, among whom I might mention: Polk, Cleburne, Preston Smith, Hardee, Breckenridge, Floyd and others.Cleburne, Polk, Hardee and Smith would frequently do me the honor of visiting my hospitals and calling on me socially whenever they could get me long enough from my work to talk to them.... General Preston Smith of Memphis, Tennessee, was a great big fellow with a great big heart. Ever since he assured me that all needing care and medical aid would have it through some hospital or individual, we were best of friends and corresponded as much as the confusion of war would allow.

Her next acquaintance with high rank was Gen. William Hardee. When she went to his headquarters to complain of the appalling condition of the sick, he greeted her quizzically, saying, "Well, my little girl, what is it you want? Have you a sick brother you want a furlough for?" to which she replied:

Yes, thousands of sick brothers, but I am not asking furloughs. I want you to come with me through the hospitals of this place and see for yourself what your men are enduring.

To my surprise he ordered his carriage and went with me at once, promising at the end of our tour of inspection to do everything he could to better the wretched state of affairs. He detailed soldiers to help clean and assist me in any way possible.

I got to know General Hardee better than any others of our distinguished Generals and always found him manly and a splendid soldier though almost womanly in the caring for his troops.

General Hardee was always saying: 'I'll drop in about breakfast time, or at your dinner hour. I want to see how you live and how you feed my men!' This he would say because our breakfast was usually in the last years of the war: rye coffee sweetened with sorghum, hard tack with occasionally a slice of baker's bread, but no meat, no butter, no eggs. I often wonder how in the world we had any strength to keep on our feet, much less to attend to our hospital duties. If I had such things as butter, eggs or meat, I felt it must go to the sick or convalescent.

One Major Peters, a soldier from Tennessee felt so bad that I would give all the best of things away that he sent me $50.00 a month (in Confederate bills) which he said was to be spent in buying something for Mrs. Newsom to eat; otherwise remittances were to be stopped.

General Hardee heard of this and came to my breakfast to see if I was living as had been reported. The dear old General was always so genial, agreeable and courteous that his visits were of the greatest benefit and blessing. He would always insist that I take a horseback ride with him every day while he was in Chattanooga. In other places he would send one of his staff to take me out for a drive. He never hesitated to show every honor and courtesy.[38]

General Hardee corresponded when not near the hospital. Here is an example illustrating his feeling toward Ella:

Estell Springs,
Nov. 15th, 1862

My Dear, Dear Friend:

I left Chattanooga without knowing precisely where my command was located.... I have a small house, known in Georgia and Florida as "two pens and a passage," which furnishes me a room for an office and a room for a chamber....

I went yesterday at Bragg's invitation to see him at Tullahoma. I found him rather gloomy but he brightened up under my genial smiles and happy looks. I shall try to make you acquainted with passing events and I send for your perusal alone a letter which I received from him today. It will give you some information which may interest you. Destroy it after reading it.

I miss your society more perhaps "than I am willing to acknowledge." As soon as I can get away I shall see you again, but this may not be for several weeks. I am always a better if not a wiser man when I am with you; for that might provoke you to say, as you did once before, that you love no one, much less the old General, and I might threaten again to commit suicide. You are a hard hearted creature. If you consulted your happiness you would marry. You are not a happy woman now.

Your brother is well, I have not seen him, but saw a gentleman who had, and conversed with him day before yesterday.

I congratulate you on being an authoress, a writer for the Illustrated Richmond News. A Piece signed "Anita" I know to be yours. Very, excellent, but of this more anon.

Your Friend,
W.J. Hardee

After the war in 1867, Mrs. Ella K. Newsom married Col. W. H. Trader, a Confederate officer who died in 1885, leaving her again a widow to struggle with life and its disappointments as best she could. But she had suffered other losses. As wife of Colonel Trader, she was the mother of several children who died in infancy. Only one child, Little Mary, was left to help console her grief. Through the aid of friends she secured a position in the Pension Office of the U.S. Government, where she worked for years. In 1898 she was found here working with impaired vision and hearing, but still possessing all of the graces and accomplishments which only the severe tragedy of real life can bestow upon people.

At this point in Mrs. Newsom's life the author Fraise J. Richard, a Northerner and veteran of the Union army became concerned that the Confederacy hadn't recognized her for her nursing accomplishments and honored her by bringing attention to her through his compelling newspaper and magazine articles. He felt that her contributions to the Confederacy had been overlooked and that she should be awarded the title of Florence Nightingale of the Southern Army for her sacrifices.

On June 9th, 1908, the Association of Medical Officers of the Army and Navy of the Confederacy at their annual reunion in Birmingham, Alabama, agreed and resolved that affirmative action was finally needed to publicly bestow upon Mrs. Ella Trader their eternal gratitude and love and the title of "Florence Nightingale of the South."

In 1913, the almost four score Mrs. Trader was destitute, blind in one eye, deaf and could no longer work. An article appeared in the *Confederate Veteran Magazine* that The United Daughters of the Confederacy planned to contribute to her maintenance and were advertising this fact and trying to gain pledges on her behalf.

In 1914 after almost 14 years Fraise Richard finally succeeded in raising enough funds to publish Mrs. Newsom's biography and collection of personal papers entitled: *The Florence Nightingale of the Southern Army.*

In 1918 the *Confederate Veteran* advertised that Mrs. Newsom was selling her book from her home on North Street in Washington, D.C. Even though incapacitated by her poor hearing and poor eyesight, Mrs. Newsom was still active and participated in the affairs of the day.[43]

The Academy Hospital in Chattanooga Tennessee.
Ella Newsom opened and operated this unit before it was
moved to Marrietta

Kennesaw House
Kennesaw House Hospital, August 1863–July 1864

Ella K. Newsom

Ella K. Newsom Trader
After the war

Notes

[1] Richard, Fraise J. *The Florence Nightingale of the Southern Army*. (New York and Baltimore:Broadway Publishing Co. 1914), 13-14.

[2] Ibid., 15.

[3] Ibid., 29.

[4] Ibid., 30.

[5] Ibid., 31.

[6] Ibid., 17.

[7] H.H. Cunningham. *Doctors in Gray: The Confederate Medical Service*. (Gloucester, MA: Peter Smith, 1970), 72.

[8] Schroeder-Lein, Glenna R. *Confederate Hospitals on the Move: Samuel H. Stout and The Army of Tennessee*. (Columbia, SC: University of South Carolina Press, 1994), 44.

[9] Richard, *The Florence Nightingale of the Southern Army*, 34-35.

[10] Cunningham, *Doctors in Gray: The Confederate Medical Service*, 72.

[11] Ibid., 73.

[12] Richard, *The Florence Nightingale of the Southern Army*, 39.

[13] Ibid., 40-41.

[14] James M. McPherson. *Ordeal by Fire: The Civil War and Reconstruction*. (New York: Alfred A. Knopf, 1982), 229.

[15] Cunningham, *Doctors in Gray. The Confederate Medical Service*, 72.

[16] Richard, *The Florence Nightingale of the Southern Army*, 44-45.

[17] Richard Harwell, ed. Kate Cumming. *Kate: The Journal of a Confederate Nurse*. (Savannah, GA: The Beehive Press, 1975), 29.

[18] Richard, *The Florence Nightingale of the Southern Army*, 46.

[19] Ibid., 45.

[20] John Wilson. *Chattanooga's Story*. Chattanooga News Press. 1980: 78.

[21] Harwell, *Kate: The Journal of a Confederate Nurse*, 53.

[22] Ibid., 65.

[23] Ibid., 65-66.

[24] Ibid., 76.

[25] Ibid., 76-77.

[26] Ibid., 77.

[27] Wilson, *Chattanooga Story*, 78.

[28] James W. Livingwood. *The Chattanooga Country: Gateway to History*. (Chattanooga, TN: Chattanooga Historical Association, 1995), 173-174.

[29] Ibid., 174.

[30] Ibid., 183.

[31] Harwell, *Kate: The Journal of a Confederate Nurse*, 85.

[32] Richard, *The Florence Nightingale of the Southern Army*, 55.

[33] Ibid., 100-101.

[34] McPherson, *Ordeal by Fire*, 338.

[35] Cobb County Federal Savings and Loan Association. *Historic Cobb County*, 21-22.

[36] *Official Records of the War of the Rebellion*, Series I, Part III, Vol. XXXVIII, 44-46.

[37] Livingwood, *The Chattanooga Country: Gateway to History*, 190.

[38] Richard, *The Florence Nightingale of the Southern Army*, 63-65.

[39] Ibid., 65.

[40] Ibid. *Confederate Veteran*, Vol. VI, 1898: 162-63.

[41] Richard, *The Florence Nightingale of the Southern Army*, 96-97.

[42] Ann Marlow. "Mrs. Ella King Newsom Trader," *Confederate Veteran*. July 1913, 342-44.

[43] Richard, "The Florence Nightingale of the Southern Army," *Confederate Veteran*, May 1918, 223.

7

THE PRISONER
The Incarceration of Mrs. Mary M. Stockton Terry

By
Jeanne M. Christie

Women who live and work in war zones experience events that change their lives, their sense of community and country. During times of national crisis like the War Between the States, radical shifts in cultural, environmental, and political structures created diverse opportunities for women's growth and development. Living in a war zone, forced women to adapt a flexible, experiential (learning by doing) style of learning that linked their development with critical social and psychological support systems. Women frequently coped with disrupted routines, and resolved problems of their survival, security and safety while alone. The residual impact lasted the duration of their lives and even affected their children.

During the War Between the States, Union soldiers enforced martial law. Charges for arrest frequently focused on providing assistance or materials to "the enemy." In many instances, the perceived enemy was a close friend or family member. Both the Confederacy and the Union took advantage of skilled, courageous women who acted as couriers, or spies appropriating official secrets. In the South, it was not uncommon for women to work as blockade runners or Confederate agents, using treachery and "feminine ways" to acquire needed supplies.[1] Survival and belief in national pride were two reasons ladies became engaged in these war activities.However, less adventurous ladies often had to demonstrate courage and use communication skills when returning home with supplies for their homes or farms. Capture or arrest required quick thinking and then a mustering of various dignitaries or family friends for release. Affluent ladies had financial resources and social abilities to help them through difficult times while ladies of decreasing status suffered during Union detainment. Women learned techniques to cope with the impending isolation of incarceration and did the best they could to survive with dignity and honor.

Esteemed ladies, such as Maryland born Rose Greenhow, were known as "a spy for the Confederacy." Rose was held under house arrest in the high profile Old Capitol Prison in Washington. Even while incarcerated she continued to send information to the Confederacy. The military eventually released her to the state of Virginia. In Virginia, President Jefferson Davis encouraged her to sail for England where she could gain support of the British, but the diligent work, ultimately cost Rose her life.[2] Other Southern women like Antoinette Gilbert 'Nettie' Slator, a.k.a. "the lady in the veil," from New Bern, North Carolina, go slightly acknowledged. Nettie worked with John Surratt successfully transporting messages through Union lines to St. Albans, Canada, until April 4, 1865, when she simply disappeared from all known sources.[3]

Ladies across the South were arrested and placed in abruptly confiscated private residences by the Union. For example, in St. Louis in 1861, political prisoners were held in private homes on Myrtle and Gratiot Street as well as at the Chestnut Street prison. Mrs. Lowden and Mrs. Lucy Nicholson Lindsay were incarcerated in the Gratiot Street prison for three weeks. They were then moved to the Chestnut Street prison where they joined at least seven other ladies. About three weeks later they were banished for "disloyalty to the Union."[4] Little is know about other women in the same location. For example, Mrs. Fanny Bauers (arrested August 12, 1862) or Ms. Laura Davis (arrested May 19, 1863) of St. Louis were also incarcerated and held at the Gratiot location. How long they remained, is not known. Other women such as Ruth and Sarah Bond (arrested April 7, 1864) of Miller County Missouri, or Anna Fickle (arrested February 22, 1864) of Lafayette County, Missouri were sent to the Myrtle Street location. Once more, their stories remain untold. Alton Prison in Illinois, was the location of confinement for Mrs. Betty Conklin. Others such as, Miss Nannie Douthill of Pocahontas, Arkansas, Miss Mollie N. Groggin of Cooper County, Missouri, and Misses Eliza J. and Rachel Haynie from Saline County, Missouri, were detained until the end of the war or until they would take a loyalty oath.

Allegiance to the Union, or to your family and community, were difficult decisions during the war. For example, Mrs. Lomax was a loyal Virginian matriarch of a well-respected family in Washington D.C. society prior to the war. She faced a dilemma between her allegiance and the social prominence that protected during the war. The protection ceased on February 2, 1863, when her daughters, Anna and Julie, were arrested and imprisoned at Old Point Prison. A third daughter, Virginia, was arrested and sent to Old Capitol Prison in Washington residing right under the room Mary Surratt would eventually occupy.[5]

Ladies of southern heritage were abused with verbal assaults and physical harassment. Some ladies refused to remain at home and chose to reside close to their husbands. While living with their husbands in the field, they were subjected to the same physical threats, hostile living conditions, and potential arrest. Occasionally, pregnant women appeared on rosters or in soldier's accounts such as the incident of a POW at Point Lookout, Maryland. A sergeant writing about the events of the day of June 11th, wrote ".... a young rebel lady prisoner in the prison has given birth to a little artilleryman." [6] Some women were arrested while visiting with their husbands' regiment and were listed on the Union rosters as female POW's such as Mrs. Martin at City Point, Virginia[7] while other women like Flora Hutzler, of Richmond, used their families mercantile business to justify her war time experiences. Frequently, family life and death transactions guided the women through turbulent times only to be snared in the web of military personalities and pride. Such was the case of Mrs. Mary M. Terry of Lynchburg, Virginia. Her incarceration sheds light on her psychological health and welfare, military personalities, and of several less fortunate women she encountered while incarcerated.

Mary was born in 1823 to the family of Dr. Ebenezer Stockton of Princeton, New Jersey. She married in 1839, at age sixteen to a Princeton student, Mr. A.W.C. Terry of Lynchburg, Virginia.[8] After the University they moved to Lynchburg to raise a family of four children. However, Mary remained close to her mother after her father's death by corresponding regularly with her and returning back home whenever possible.

In May of 1864, Mrs. Mary Terry and Miss Rowena C. Selden, a traveling companion, had gone to Point of Rocks, Virginia, located on the Appomatox River where it joins the James River. Upon arrival at Point of Rocks they asked permission from the Union commanding officer, Colonel Schley, to pass through the lines to Baltimore. Their request was granted and they proceeded north. In Baltimore the two women followed protocol and reported to Colonel Fish the Provost Marshall. Miss Selden remained with friends in town, while Mrs. Terry continued to her mother's in Princeton, New Jersey.

Mrs. Terry purchased many new clothes and materials in preparation to return to Virginia and headed back to Baltimore. Aware of the war-time situation and protocol, Mary followed standard procedures and gathered appropriate authorizations, invoices and lists, to pass the Custom House in Baltimore. The three trunk contents and military forms were submitted to Colonel Fish. He personally examined the trunks to make sure they matched the invoices. Mary was informed that she would be permitted to take her belongings and pass through the lines the next morning. About nine o'clock in the evening, there was a knock at the door of the residence Mrs. Terry was lodging in. The soldiers arrested Mrs. Terry. The Union claimed right to everything she had with her other than the clothes on her body. The next morning she was allowed to pass through the lines without a trunk, a package, a bag or the slightest additional piece of clothing or supplies. Mary was furious. General Schenck informed her that if she tried to go through with all the excess goods again, he would arrest her as spy and blockade runner.

Outraged with anger but cognizant of her rights, Mrs. Terry sought political friends. A suit was filed in the U.S. Court system before Judge Giles who helped Mary recover the goods from General Schenck, Colonel Fish and friends. The initial estimated value was for two thousand dollars, however, six hundred dollars of silk dresses were unaccounted for and rumored to have been seen on General Schenck's wife and his lady friends.

Several months later Mrs. Terry lost her second husband.[9] As Executrix she found it necessary to pass through Union lines to reach New York in order to settle his estate and banking affairs. Understanding the anger and vindictive nature of General Schenck and Colonel Fish, Mrs. Terry sought alternate routes to reach New York. She remained in the city until the arrangements were satisfactory and all banking was in order.

Several months had transpired between the first incident and the return trip home. Mrs. Terry believed traveling back through Baltimore to be safe but she wanted to recover dresses that had mysteriously reappeared, although they had received some wear and tear. Mary had no indication to suspect events were unsettled with the General and Colonel. Unaware of the festering problem, she went out to the Eastern Shore of Maryland "to help with some children of family friends" from the Princess Anne area. The area was known for Southern sympathizers, and as a point to cross the river and run the blockade. Mary had two large travel trunks, a hand carried box, plus the recovered items. Local Union sympathizers informed a government detective who arrested her on May 28th. Mary was charged with having too many goods and planning to run the blockade. She was returned to Baltimore and charged for being a blockade-runner and a spy. Mary was taken to the home of Mrs. Emmerich who lived on Lombard Street in the city.[10] After examining the evidence in a trial for nine days, the charges were dropped.

Concerned about the impending length of return and baggage logistics Mary felt she needed assistance. She wrote a letter to General Wallace, asking desire for his assistance to have the goods sent to the children in Virginia.[11] It was for writing to the General, and the wish of sending goods to Virginia, that Mrs. Terry was sentenced to close confinement for a one-year period in Salem, Massachusetts.[12]

Mary's diary during her incarceration, reveals a great deal about the experiences she survived. The diary divulges how she learned to handle the harassment and abuse. The progressive entries described the breaking internal values and beliefs by the Union guards. Compared to women who had to sleep in the dungeon, survive on prison fare, or were unable to communicate with outside support systems, Mary's incarceration seemed easy. She had money for food and was allowed mail, newspapers, and packages while in prison. Her accommodations were on the second floor in a room away from the normal cells. Initially, Mary was able to hire a less fortunate prison girl, to clean her linens and the floors. What she did not have was sufficient heat when the weather turned cold, people to talk with who were like her, and privacy from invasive public visitors.

As comfortable as Mary was, incarceration was very traumatic for her. An illustration can be seen as the diary begins on May 28, 1864. Under threat of death she is taken to Mrs. Emmerich's house by four guards. Mary is confined to the house without any food for two days. On the third, fourth and fifth[13] day she is allowed prison food but without any meat. An opportunity to purchase strawberries from a vendor outside of her window, is squelched and Mrs. Terry becomes very angry with the Yankees and wishes that "a ball finds them." On June 21, Captain Skinner informs Mrs. Terry that she is to be transferred in two hours. Depressed and angry, Mary comments that she feels too ill to move. Angered by her audacity and insolence Colonel Woolley threatens her. Even in a depressed state of mind, she experiences a coping solution that will help her survive the long months ahead. Mustering courage not to comply with their verbal abuse, instantaneous demands and threats, Mrs. Terry counters with a reply. "If they want to go they [the Captain] will have to dress me, comb my hair, and lift me from my bed."[14] Shocked that a woman would have the composure to demand anything, Captain Skinner complied. Mrs. Terry had learned a source of pleasure and control that she would use while a prisoner. Her journey North started at six o'clock in the evening. Transportation arrangements became confused and the Captain had to take her to a Hotel to wait for the train. While waiting for the train, she observed a role model that formulated Mary's values during her own war with the Union. At the Hotel, a Mrs. Granby refused to leave by walking under the flag of the Union. Pleased by what she had seen, Mrs. Terry remarked "Ah, she was good metal"[15] which meant she had good values. Her ethics and standards had become clear, setting the stage for other decisions to come. The ability to cope with the adversity had begun to fall in line.

Moving north meant that the military had to billet Mrs. Terry in a variety of locations. Reaching New York City, too late to catch the train for Boston, required a stay at the Nicholas Hotel. Her husband's old friends were contacted and came to see her. Mrs. Terry reinforced her support system and asserted her dignity and pride by dressing in her best attire. Under a relaxed guard she was permitted to spend the evening in the hotel parlor with a dear friend, Mr. Ned Halsey. She clearly saw her duty of upholding the concept of a lady, unbending to the Yankee forces and understood her self worth when she wrote that she "did not choose to make myself miserable because [she] was a prisoner."[16] The next day was very hot and dusty train-ride to Boston.

On June 25, 1864 they reached Salem, Massachusetts and reported to Capt. Daniel Johnson at the Provost Marshal's Office. Having no accommodation for ladies, the Captain sent Mrs. Terry to the boarding house of Mrs. Woodbury as a temporary woman's prison. In Salem Mary experienced being inspected by the native population's eyes and minds as they gathered to see the rebel prisoner. Without proper prison accommodations, the officers in charge felt compelled to occupy her time. They collectively toured the towns of Beverly and Salem, purchased ice cream, and even went to a dramatization of Milton's Paradise Lost at the Mechanic Hall. On June 30, Captain Skinner received orders to return back to Baltimore with Mrs. Terry. Life of a prisoner appeared more of an inconvenience, than a trial of endurance for Mrs. Terry.

Jail in Baltimore was basic but not forever. Mary wrote to Colonel Woolley for permission to walk about the garden in the morning and evening. Mail was permitted, she was not far from friends, but felt lost when the key was turned in the door bolt. She drew courage and strength from her trust in God and felt she needed to be content with her life and look for peace within herself. She knew she had small blessings such as food, a table, chair and bed, a window to look out, and a woman for a warden. She was pleased that she could hear the church bells and created pleasant images in her mind when she heard the bells ring.

Recursion of her earlier learning experience transpired when she was told she would move again. She thought about how her demand for information had helped her obtain what she had needed. She fussed a bit and made another successful assertive demand.

She stated that she would "not go one step [farther] until [she] knew to what point."[17] This time the destination was to Fitchburg, Massachusetts. Once more, Captain Skinner escorted Mrs. Terry, arriving in New York City with a four-hour layover. With no carriage available the Captain demands she get out and walk with him. Once more, a point of arguing with the Union authority proved to have been a wise learning experience. Thirty minutes of arguing and informing him of the inappropriateness of his demand for a lady to walk the streets of the city, the Captain arranged for a carriage. She had won another victory. At Fitchburg, Mary was turned over to the warden of the Worcester County House of Correction. Mrs. Terry seizes the opportunity to speak her mind to Captain Skinner. With a sharp tongue she offers some advice on behavior, ethics, and governmental position. She said, "he has shown his patriotism escorting innocent women to prison."[18]

In Salem on the first trip north, she had the Captain and his wife to talk with. But in Fitchburg, she had endless hours to sit or walk in solitude. In the County House of Correction she was allowed regular mail and walks in the prison yard but isolation was the order of the day. Finally, Mary conversed with several of the other women, especially two women who are from the South, and in great need. On March 25 information about the women ran in the Fitchburg Sentinel: "We have learned that two rebels of the female persuasion arrived in Boston on Tuesday last...The ladies (?) are said to be ardent secessionists and they will undoubtedly find ready sympathy with their "wayward sisters" who were imprisoned in the same place several months since."[19]

Mary tried to build their morale and help them to read but her spirit becomes crushed and her soul seems lost within. Entries in her diary become random and she is depressed. Limitations of her faith, the fate that lies before her, plus her decreasing congenial spirit, tax her mind. She begins to hear voices and realizes that she is reading and speaking loudly just to hear the human voice.

Adding insult to injury, the Yankees visit the jail to view the rebels like a sideshow in a circus. This offended and greatly angered her especially when she is forced to appear for the visitors' review.

Mary refused and expressed that she could make money by charging one dollar if the Yankees want to see what she looks like. Her remarks infuriate the wardens and she is confined to her room.However, her animosity toward the touring parties prompted a spark of old self-affirmation in her ability to hold a conversation. She talked with other prisoners and decided to play psychological games with the touring parties and limited staff. Mrs. Terry realized that even gallows humor might help them survive. Mary was considerate of those around her and expressed the feeling that life was bleak, but others were in more difficult situations. For example, some women had limited skills or cultured background than she had. Several of the women's houses had been burned to the ground and there were men who had been shot or were infested with bugs and were just lying about.[20] At one point, she violated a prison rule by speaking to several men and was punished. She empathized when others were punished and mourned quietly when she heard of family problems at home or losses for the Confederacy.

Living alone was difficult for Mrs. Terry. On August 2, 1864, Mrs. Sawyer, was transferred from Old Capitol Prison.[21] They became close friends and shared many secrets, stories and supplies. With the new psychological shift Mary felt stronger and decided to "go to the office to be viewed" by the Yankees. Angered by their attitude and outraged that nothing had changed, she noted in the diary "so much comes from being with low down Yankees that know not that there is such a thing as refinement in the world." [22] The incident so unsettled her that she lost perspective of the reality that held her together for so many months.

During the early incarceration, Mrs. Terry had learned to be positive and amusing despite the negative environment. She had beliefs and coping mechanisms that sustained her mental health and encouraged her spirit. As winter approached, the prison environment was taking its toll. One day with her psychological guard down[23] she engaged in a heated dialog with Mrs. Nicholas the warden. She noted in her diary that she "had a blowout with Mrs. Nicholas this morning. She (Mrs. Nicholas) spoke to me like I was a negro, and I do not choose for her, or anyone else to speak to me in a dictatorial manner, [I] informed her it was not to be done again."[24] Having confronted the authority figure and being insulted in front of other prisoners, Mary retreated into a shell. Life seemed bleak and hopeless, the weather was cold and her only consoling warmth was to stay in bed or sleep.She submitted to the harassment and demoralizing displays by the warden but she would not submit to the touring Yankees unless forced into the situation. She found insulting them was worth it if she could do so. Diary entries about incoming mail or personal ads she had seen in the papers are reduced. She feels life is very monotonous, one day goes on like another.[25] The months continue on but one of her last entries indicates the strength of conviction and courage that ran deeply through her mental makeup. Without family or friends to assist her she grows despondent and directs anger inward by wishing that she had more faith in God and a stronger sense of religion. Life seems incredibly bleak. For the next few days she makes no entries and is unable to even put pen to paper.

There is little information about Mrs. Terry after imprisonment. Her term of incarceration ended on May 21, 1865 and she was released. It is not clear if she remained in New Jersey until the war ended or if she headed back to Virginia.[26] While incarcerated at Fitchburg, Mrs. Terry made notation about other women who were in the facility. Some are only names such as Mrs. Munrow from Suffolk, Virginia,[27] whose house was burned by the Yankee's while others offer the dates and reasons for their arrests. They are as follows: On July 28, 1864, Mrs. Margaret Murphy, Southern prisoner but no location given, but she had been here 2 years and five months. September 21, 1864, two women prisoners came in from Washington for assisting a Union soldier to desert. They were each sentenced for six months. September 28, 1864, two women counterfeiters, sentenced for nine months. October 6, 1864, another woman is sent to Fitchburg from Washington and sentenced to one year. October 17, 1864, Ms. Jane Perkins from Danville, Pittsylvannia County Virginia arrives. December 29, 1984, Mrs. Terry was moved next to Mrs. Hutchings, who was from Baltimore, Maryland. She had been sentenced to five years and a $5,000.00 fine.[28]

The details of the lives of women who had to endure the war has been generalized or overlooked for generations. The burdens they carried during the war years and the experiences they endured may never be fully explored. Historians write about the men of Andersonville but rarely discuss Alton and Elmira.[29] They analyze war and the movements on maps. They write about how the war effected "everyone" but rarely focus on the perspective of women who fought the war with their heart and soul, and intellect. The war provided women with lifelong learning opportunities and a commitment to share the education with future generations.Incarceration of Southern women provided them with a depth of understanding of what they were truly capable of, that few Northern women could even imagine. Heroic deeds and actions of Southern women created admirable role models for the future generations. Their tenacious patriotic spirits, and inspirational vision, fostered future advocates for women's rights in the years following the war. They would appear soft and gracious on the outside but focused and determined to survive on the inside, regardless of what happened in their lives.

Fitchburg County Jail

County jail at south Fitchburg, Massachusetts. Women sympathetic to the South were jailed here. Note women on lower veranda.

Notes

[1] J.M. Christie. "Learning Patterns of Women in Virginia." Unpublished manuscript. 1994. University of Connecticut.

[2] She was returning to the States on September 30, 1864 via a block-ade runner when the steamer ran aground and her lifeboat capsized in heavy seas. Rose carried heavy gold sovereigns that pulled her under. Her body washed ashore on October 1, 1864. R. Larson. *Blue and Gray Roses of Intrigue*, (Gettysburg: Thomas Publications, 1993); I. Ross. *Rebel Rose: The Life of Rose O'Neal Greenhow, Confederate Spy*, (Marietta, GA: Mockingbird Books, 1954).

[3] J.M. Christie. "No Place For a Woman": The Lives of Women at City Point, Virginia, 1864-1865. Research and exhibit for National Park Service exhibit.March 1994; J.O. Hall. "The Lady in the Veil." *The Maryland Independent.* June 25, 1975. LaPlata, Maryland.

[4] Mrs. Tyler Floyd. Reminiscences of Mrs. Lucy Nickolson Lindsay. *Reminiscences of the Civil War: Women of Missouri During the Sixties.* (St. Louis: United Daughters of the Confederacy, 1929).

[5] Mrs. Lomax had three daughters who were picked up and impris-oned at Old Point prison and Old Capitol Prison toward the end of the war. Mrs. Elizabeth Virginia (Lindsay) Lomax. Lomax Papers. The Virginia State Historical Society, Richmond, Va.; L.L. Wood, Ed., Leaves From An Old Washington Diary, 1854-1863. (New York: E.P. Dutton & Co., 1943).

[6] Diary of "Sergeant J. Jones, Point Lookout POW." June 11, 1864. Probably Pvt. Jane A. Perkins of Danville, Virginia who fought with the Spotsylvania Artillery. Per conversation with Edwin Beitzell, Point Lookout Prison Camp for Confederates, Saint Mary's County Historical Society.

[7] In January, 1865, Provost Marshal Patrick's diary refers to Mrs. Martin at City Point, Virginia, waiting as a POW to be sent through

the lines back to Mobile, Alabama. Transcribed diary notes of Marsena Patrick, National Park Service, City Point, Virginia.

[8] Abner Wentworth Clopton Terry, born at Danville, VA in 1815, died in Lynchburg, Virginia, on June 8, 1851. Family notes. The Virginia State Historical Society.

[9] Abner Wentworth Clopton Terry was shot to death in 1851. Family notes indicate Mary married S. Dexter Otey in 1853. Otey had been employed by a bank in New York City as a cashier. He was referred to by Ryan during the trial as a husband who had been less than discrete and killed in an "encounter" by a Naval Officer name Lyons the year before. National Archives and Records Administration, Court Martial file MM1466; Personal notes from Miss E.S. West, Terry file, The Virginia State Historical Society, 1954.

[10] Mrs. Emmerich was a woman who had been sympathetic to the South and so the military appropriated her home and turned it into a women's prison for at least five months. Mrs. Terry's personal diary, The Virginia State Historical Society.

[11] Two of her children of the first marriage had died, the others were grown by the war years. The only child of the second marriage had died in 1856. Mary had extended family in Virginia. She carried over $2,000 worth of goods in her baggage.

[12] Terry left Baltimore June 23, 1864 and was transported to Salem, Massachusetts, where there were no accommodations for female prisoners. She returned to Baltimore June 30, then moved back to Massachusetts and placed in the Worcester County House of Correction in Fitchburg. She was charged with four counts. The first charge was for acting as a spy. The government failed to convict her on the first three counts. She was convicted on the fourth as being within the 8th Army Corps lines in Maryland, contrary to the orders of the commanding general. Information per Fitchburg. Historical Society.

[13] These dates would have been June 6-8, 1864. Mary Terry's diary.

[14] Ibid., June 21.

[15] Ibid.

[16] Ibid.

[17] Ibid.

[18] Ibid.

[19] The other women, Murphy, Johnson and Perkins had particularly turbulent dispositions. Perkins had caused a considerable amount of noise and had been threatened with the dark cell. She had to be placed in iron cuffs upon her wrists, in the dungeon for two days. Personal diary July 25, 1864; *Fitchburg Sentinel*, March 25, 1864.

[20] The Worcester *DailySpy* states that there were 34 persons in the jail and the House of Correction for December 1864. About 20 of them were women and twelve specifically named as Mary Murphy, Annie E. Jones, Mary Jane Johnson, Sarah E. Monroe, Mary S. Terry, Mary E. Sawyer, Rebecca Smith, Maria Kelley, Elizabeth Buckley, Jane A. Perkins, Sarah Mitchell and Sarah Hutchins.

[21] Mrs. Sawyer, age 34, arrived on August 3, 1864 and was discharged August 18. She was a well educated and politically connected member of Baltimore. She was charged and incarcerated for corresponding with the enemy from the city of Baltimore. Her husband was serving in the Confederate army. Information provided by Fitchburg Historical Society.

[22] Personal diary of Mary Terry.

[23] Ibid., August 10, 1864.

[24] Ibid., August 10, 1864.

[25] Ibid.

[26] Turner Baker Papers. Record Group 94, file T3970. National Archives and Records Administration.

[27] Mrs. Munrow's husband was killed while serving in the Confederate army. She was 27, and lived two miles from the Spotsylvania battlefield.

She was arrested, leaving her elderly mother and four children standing in the yard. Mrs. Munrow was charged with harboring Confederate soldiers and guerillas. Worcester *Daily Spy*. August 23, 1864; Terry diary July 13, 1864.

[28] Mary Murphy was an uneducated woman who was trying to learn to read. She occasionally refused the wardens orders and was hit in the face and/or sent to reside in the dungeon. Personal diary [See footnote 19]. Mary Murphy is the first woman prisoner sent to the House of Correction, on November 23, 1863. She was arrested for purchasing and then attempting to set a bridge on fire. When examined in Washington, she claimed that her name was Mrs. Jefferson Davis. Fitchburg Historical Society; Terry Diary. Probably Rebecca Smith and Maria Kelley, both age twenty, who arrived on September 24, 1864. They were arrested for abetting soldiers to desert and furnishing them with citizen's clothes. The *Worcester Daily Spy*. Fitchburg Historical Society.

[29] The Fitchburg *Sentinel* includes a variety of entries for 1864 reporting trains of Southern soldiers being sent to Elmira, New York. Any individual who took pity on the prisoners and attempted to give them food or clothing was locked in the car and taken to Elmira for abetting the enemy.

8

THE POETESS
Margaret Junkin Preston of Lexington, Virginia

By
William H. Baria, M.D.

Her friends in the town of Lexington, Virginia called the little lady "Maggie". Margaret Junkin, daughter of Washington College's antebellum president Dr. George Junkin, was a Pennsylvanian by birth, and a Southerner by choice. By an unwelcome twist of fate, she and Julia were the surviving sister to Eleanor, known as "Ellie" the ill-fated first wife of Gen. Thomas J. "Stonewall" Jackson.

Although the smallish, auburn haired Margaret battled an inflamed eye condition throughout her adult life, she managed to create poetry which reached the heart of the war torn South. Such poems as "Beechenbrook" earned Maggie the title of "The Poetess of the Confederacy." However Margaret's dedicated service to her loved ones took precedence over her pen.

In 1857, at age 37 Margaret married Maj. J. T. L. Preston, a widower with seven children. This union, which produced two sons, proved the ideal marriage for Maggie for the Major was a man of deep religious conviction and forceful character. This Virginian, a teacher of Latin and classics at the Virginia Military Institute, helped found the college with Col. Francis Smith. Major Preston availed himself of one of the best educations obtainable in the antebellum era. He studied at Washington College, University of Virginia, and Yale. With the advent of Civil War, Preston rose to the rank of colonel as a valuable member of General Jackson's staff.

Maggie's courage matched her problems. The rearing of seven step children and two natural sons wasn't an easy task as her diary suggests. Mrs. Bryan, a Preston granddaughter wrote, "My mother was a little girl of seven or eight at this time and stood loyally by the new mama while the older children treated her coolly, as was the fashion of the day."

Mrs. Preston, a lady in print, had to overcome other prejudices of the day. Colonel Preston took his new bride to meet his aristocratic Virginia family at "Oakland" on the James River where she won the approval of Col. William C. Preston, a famed South Carolina orator. This statesman had shared the prevailing attitude in the South of disapproving of women in print. His feelings changed from those of disfavor of "this little red headed yankee with want of style and presence" to "she is an encyclopedia in small print."

Another note written by Mrs. Bryan was enlightening. "I once heard Gen. Lee's daughter, Miss Mary, say that she w'd publish her travels & journals (both of unusual interest) but for her brother Gen. Custis Lee's objection to seeing the women of the family in print!"

Maggie could count on her husband's unwavering support of her creative efforts throughout the coming years. Margaret's broad literary knowledge, personal integrity, and talent was exceeded only by her unselfish devotion to the well being of those entrusted to her care. Maggie won the well deserved trust and affection of her adopted family.

Superimposed upon these career difficulties were the horrors and deprivations of the Civil War. Internal conflicts arose in many southern families. Dr. Junkin erupted as a stormy petrel whenever anyone challenged his avid belief in the union of North and South. Maggie was among those members of Junkin's large family who felt the backwash of his encounters. Dr. Junkin's other opinions, such as the gradual abolishment of slavery instead of its sudden abolition, produced difficulties in Pennsylvania, and contributed to his accepting the Washington College presidency in 1849.

The good Presbyterian advocated the recolonization of Africa by ex-slaves who wished to return to their homeland, and proposed that Congress should foot the bill to the tune of five million dollars. Dr. Junkin believed these returnees would serve as instruments to Christianize the African continent.

The Junkin family's honeymoon existence with Washington College ended approximately ten years later when the drums of secession began to beat. The flag of "disunion" with its red star flew above the wooden head of George Washington from one of the campus buildings. Maggie and the Junkin family remained in Lexington at great peril. Violence threatened in the once tranquil town. On one occasion, a cook was alleged to have poisoned the family's food after the entire family suffered a severe intestinal illness. Following a series of angry flag snatching incidents, Dr. Junkin issued an ultimatum to students and trustees. He would not teach another class if the "disunion" flag flew over the campus. The flag flew, and the board of trustees accepted Dr. Junkin's resignation without regret.

Maggie knew how to endure heartbreak. Her father with two sons and daughter Julia, returned to Pennsylvania. This scholarly Presbyterian minister had helped found Lafayette College, and had served as president of Miami of Ohio.

Now the tight knit Junkin family, originally of twelve children, was ripped apart. The good doctor left behind in addition to Maggie the graves of his wife and his daughter Eleanor. Two sons would join the Confederate Army.

Legend holds that Dr. Junkin drove the last thirty five miles out of Virginia without feeding his horses. The educator stopped in the Potomac River to wash the dust of Virginia off of his feet before crossing over into Maryland.

Margaret had tasted the bitter anguish of separation caused by death. Her sister Ellie, wife of Thomas Jonathan Jackson, died in childbirth in 1854. Her cherished mother passed in the same year leaving Maggie to mother the Junkin family. The pain of the wartime family separation was eased somewhat when Maggie, with General Jackson's help, managed to correspond with her father and sister, Julia, in Pennsylvania.

Then came that Sunday in May of 1863 when the storied Stonewall Jackson succumbed at Guinea Station to his wounds. The battlefield genius' letters to Margaret had read like those of a warm brother. This stern General expressed tender feelings to Margaret concerning the happenings of the day that he probably discussed only with his wife.

Margaret Junkin Preston braced for the gathering storm. The terrible reality of war touched the Preston Home. Colonel Preston's son Frank, a Confederate soldier, returned to the Preston home in Lexington after amputation of his arm. Mrs. Bryan makes note of the fact that this event constituted an awful family tragedy. Frank had been a gifted violinist.

Margaret's emotions stemmed from her confrontations with life's tragedies. Maggie helped support her husband through his anguish after the Colonel uncovered his son Wily's mangled body from a crude grave on the battlefield following the second battle of Manassas. Margaret existed first of all as a wife, a consoler and defender of her family, a preserver of scarce vegetables, jams and jellies, and lastly a fine poetess.

The war swept into Lexington on June 10, 1864. Gen. David Hunter's Union Army shelled the defenseless town and on the next day his men plundered the village. Hunter ordered V.M.I. burned along with Governor Letcher's homestead. The invaders wantonly destroyed books, laboratory equipment, and furnishings at Washington College. Margaret saved scant foodstuffs from marauding, gun wielding Federals to feed Confederate wounded. She hid slabs of bacon under her front steps. The Preston home served as a refuge in the ravaged town.

Maggie shared great risks with the other residents of Lexington. Her house might have been burned during General Hunter's occupation of the town if the late Stonewall Jackson's sword had been discovered in her attic. This weapon was later hidden in the piano Jackson had bought for his second wife, Mary Anna Morrison.

Mrs. Preston's poetry reached out to comfort hurting Southerners who needed solace, and etched in the memories of those suffering people the devotion to duty and the valor of their slain loved ones. Many a cherished family member had been wrapped in a blanket and buried in a shallow, unmarked grave on a far flung battlefield.

Maggie scorned the idea that she wrote for posterity. She referred to herself as "a singer with a slender trill." The world knew better. Margaret's poem brought tears to the eyes of the hardened soldiers when Colonel Preston read aloud the lines of "Beechenbrook":

"Only A Private"

Only a private;—and who would care
When I may pass away,—
Or how, or why I perish, or where
I mix with the common clay?
They will fill my empty place again
With another as bold and brave;
And they'll blot me out ere the Autumn rain
Has freshened my nameless grave.

One of the last verses of Beechenbrook needs reading:

Only a private;—yet He who reads
Through the guises of the heart,
Looks not at the splendor of the deeds,
But the way we do our part;
And when He shall take us by the hand,
And our small service own,
There'll be a glorious band of privates stand
As victors around the throne!

Colonel Preston received the manuscript on the rough dark paper, and Richmond printers published the poem in dim type. Only a handful of the 2,000 original copies escaped the flames of the burning Confederate Capital. Fortunately for posterity, the poem was republished in Baltimore in 1866.

Margaret continued to write in spite of her failing vision, and carried on a vigorous correspondence. The poetess wasn't dismayed. She had spent seven years in her early life in the semidarkness. The poetess' lyrical verses sang again the dying words of Generals Lee and Jackson in "Gone Forward" and "The Shade Of The Tree." The first verse of "Gone Forward" reads:

Yes. "Let the tent be struck." victorious morning
Through every crevice flashes in a day

Magnificent beyond all earth's adorning:
The night is over; wherefore should he stay?
And wherefore should our voices choke to say,
"The General has gone forward"?

Maggie enshrined the dying Stonewall Jackson's last words in
her poem "The Shade Of The Trees:"

What are the thoughts that are stirring in his breast?
What is the mystical vision he sees?
'Let us pass over the river and rest
Under the shade of the trees.'

Margaret concluded the poem:

Yea, it is noblest for him – it is best,
(Questioning naught of our Father's decrees)
There to pass over the river and rest
Under the shade of the trees!

These words didn't represent abstract lines by a fawning poet.
Margaret hurt. She grieved with the families of both great men.
Maggie possessed a deep sisterly love for her slain brother-in-law,
wept at the passing of his first wife, sister Ellie, and remained a trusted friend to Mary Anna Jackson.

Did Maggie know Mary Lee's thwarted ambition to write?
She shared the Lee family's post-war tribulations when Mrs. Lee
became an invalid. Death carried away not only the General but his
daughter, Agnes. Margaret wrote a poem a month after gracious
Agnes Lee's passing. The last verse of "Agnes" reads:

Ah, can we live and bear to truss
Out of our lives this life so rare?
Tender, so tender! an angel's kiss
Hallowed it daily, unaware;
Gracious as sunshine, sweet as dew

Shut in a lily's golden core,
Fragrant with goodness through and through,
Pure as the spikenard Mary bore;
Holy as twilight soft as dawn,
Agnes has gone!

Mrs. Bryan made this notation by the poem. "This poem was written after the death of Gen. Lee's daughter Agnes – a warm friend of Mrs. Preston's."

Margaret struggled with the relationship of her personal career to family duties. She expressed career regrets while visiting Mrs. Bryan's home in Maryland. When the Bryan child's father called, the hostess immediately dropped her housework.

"My dear, have you time to go?" remarked Maggie.

"Yes," replied Mrs. Bryan. "When my husband wants me I have time for nothing else."

Margaret sadly remarked, "I wish I had always been as wise."

Margaret Junkin Preston survived the degradation of her adopted homeland as the Civil War ground to a halt. Her spirit was often tested but never crushed. She recorded in her diary that Mrs. Lee, although confined to a wheelchair, remained cheerful in spirit. Margaret corresponded with other members of the literary world, the most notable being Longfellow, Whittier, and the Rosettis. After Colonel Preston resigned his teaching position at V.M.I. in 1882 the Prestons traveled in Europe. Margaret drank in the aura of all the places her literary mind longed to taste.

The Colonel and his beloved wife became inseparable companions who faced the inevitable failing years of old age together. Margaret battled failing vision, impaired hearing, and much like Mrs. Lee, was confined to a wheelchair. However until 1888 the couple spent several months each summer at McDonogh School outside Baltimore.

Margaret and the Colonel resided at the home of Col. William Allan when visiting Baltimore. William Allan's wife was the last remaining Preston daughter. Col. J.T.L. Preston passed to a final rest in his beloved home in Lexington. Margaret Junkin Preston made her way to the home in Baltimore of her eldest son, Dr. George Preston. There on March 29, 1897 the long life of this devoted wife of Colonel Preston ended. Dr. J. A. Harrison wrote a fitting epitaph for her. "Woman. Poet. Saint." Only one more word needed adding . . . "Wife."

Margaret Junkin Preston

BIBLIOGRAPHY

Allan, Elizabeth. *Life and Letters of Margaret Junkin Preston* (New York: Houghton, Mifflin, and Company, 1903).

Allan, Elizabeth Preston. *Margaret Junkin Preston [1820-1897]*, Library Of Southern Literature Volume X (Martin And Hoyt Co., 1909).

Bryan, Mrs. Personal notations recorded in pencil in the *Life And Letters Of Margaret Junkin Preston*, 1969.

Crenshaw, Ollinger. *General Lee's College* (New York: Random House, 1969).

Douglas, Henry Kyd. *I Rode With Stonewall* (Chapel Hill: University of North Carolina, 1940).

Flood, Charles Bracelen. *Lee, The Last Years* (New York: Houghton, Mifflin and Co., 1981).

Kane, Harnett T. *The Gallant Mrs. Stonewall* (New York: Doubleday & Co., 1957).

9

THE CARETAKER OF THE DEAD
Mary Amarinthia Yates Snowden of Charleston, SC

By
June Murray Wells

Mary Amarinthia Yates was born in Charleston, South Carolina on September 10, 1819, the daughter of Joseph Yates and Elizabeth Ann Saylor. Her father died when she was only eighteen months old but Mary Amarinthia was raised with her sister and two brothers by a strong and financially secure mother.

In 1857 Amarinthia married Dr. William Snowden. She bore him a son and a daughter but she was widowed at a young age during the War Between the States. The remainder of Mrs. Snowden's long life would be devoted to the Confederacy and the memory of its dead. During the war she worked diligently at clothing and feeding Confederate troops, caring for the wounded and dying, and commemorating the valiant dead.

Among her many accomplishments connected to the Confederacy, the most important was Mrs. Snowden's work as self-appointed caretaker of the Confederate dead. After the Battle of Secessionville, those who fell or who afterwards died in hospitals were provided with graves in one part of Magnolia Cemetery. Those who had lived in or close to Charleston were buried by their families in family plots and church graveyards. The dead who were received in this part of Magnolia were Confederates from many states who had been fighting together. It thus became a nucleus of a Confederate cemetery, and continued to be used for that purpose during the war. The graves were marked, as far as possible with name, rank, state and branch of service.

In 1866 Mrs. Snowden organized the Ladies' Memorial Association to take care of the Confederate dead. The city of Charleston was still in ruins from the shelling and many of those men who had died during the war had been quickly buried without ceremony in the newly established Magnolia Cemetery. Just one year after the war ended, Mrs. Snowden and her ladies held the first

Confederate Memorial Day in Charleston. It lasted from early morning until night.

Early that morning, the ladies, accompanied by Express Wagons, went around the city collecting wreaths, bouquets and garlands of flowers made by the citizens. They then separated into groups who went to the different church yards and placed flowers on each soldier's grave.

Shortly before noon all of the stores on King, Meeting, Broad, East Bay and other commercial district streets began closing. There was almost a total suspension of business in the city. By 1:00 p.m. all of the line omnibuses, hired and private carriages and other vehicles, were continually filled by crowds on their way to witness the memorial at Magnolia. At the Anne Street Depot of the South Carolina Railroad, long trains of cars, kindly donated for the event, were constantly filled and disembarked of passengers.

Long before the appointed hour of 5:00 pm for the ceremony to begin, a large mass had gathered around the Confederate lot at Magnolia, where between six and seven hundred Confederate soldiers were buried. Many of those in attendance were former soldiers themselves, and many ladies were still dressed in deep mourning. There were all classes of citizens, young and old. Also present was a black man who had lost an arm fighting for the Confederate cause at Secessionville.

At 5:00, a procession started, led by Mayor P.C. Gaillard with Mrs. Mary Amarinthia Snowden. Then came Rep. C.H. Simonton, Speaker of the House of Representatives, three ministers, Reverends Gadsden, Bowman, and W.B. Yates, the choir, and the "Garland Committee", dressed in white muslin dresses, complete with mourning collars, neck ties and belts, and wearing a badge on the left shoulder of black ribbon adorned with a miniature palmetto tree.

Representative Simonton conducted the program. First to speak was Reverend Yates who had been chaplain to the Confederate seamen. He spoke of the blessed privilege of being gathered there in safety and peace to finally pay tribute to the Southern dead who gave their lives on both land and sea. At the conclusion of the prayer, the choir sang, accompanied by Professor O'Neale at the melodeon.

Rev. John L. Girardeau, himself a former Confederate chaplain, called it a sacred spot with no political complexion, a place to express grief over both the loss and admiration for the memories of these men. He spoke of the families who had been left behind, and reminded those gathered that these men had died for them and their belief in constitutional liberty. He then related several stories of his personal experiences with dying soldiers, and became so emotional he had to change the subject. He spoke of the ladies' wartime contributions and how fitting it was that "the same hands should gently lay upon his last resting place the touching memorials of a people's gratitude and love."

The choir sang the Ode written for this occasion by native poet Henry Timrod, who died that same year. Reverend Bowman emphasized that one of the distinguishing characteristics of Christianity is to teach a reverence and respect for the ashes and tombs of the dead. He spoke of the debt of gratitude owed to the men who left their homes and came to defend those in Charleston. He mentioned the one good thing: these men had not had to deal with the humiliation of losing the war and being controlled by their conquerors. His eulogy was followed by the ode "Tears and Flowers" during which the ladies decorated each grave with bouquets. The tears indeed flowed freely, not only from the eyes of these fair daughters, but also from the eyes of many of the surviving companions of the heroic dead.

The dense crowds dispersed at dusk, and stepping aboard trains, returned to the city. Thus concluded the first memorial service, a complete success. Mrs. Snowden was now ready for a new project. She personally visited many battlefields and arranged for the removal of the dead. Her new challenge was Gettysburg and the many South Carolina soldiers buried there. Obtaining the bodies from Gettysburg was not an easy task. With papers full of notations on locations such as barns, cherry, apple or peach trees, and fences or streams, she undertook this tremendous task. Sometimes there were records of as many as nine men buried quickly side by side by comrades in one long deep grave, with a board cover and dirt on top. Mrs. Snowden went personally to find these men, and bring home their remains. Most had been buried on the battlefield and the owners of the ground refused to permit the bodies to be removed unless they were paid.

The farmers finally signed a contract with Mrs. Snowden, stating that the soldiers could be sent to Charleston in boxes furnished for $3.25 each, a portion of which was to be paid in advance. They were shipped to Baltimore where Messrs. Mordecai and Company, agents for a line of steamers between that city and Charleston, gave the boxes containing the bodies free freight costs to Charleston. It was deemed advisable at Baltimore to place the bodies on the steamer at night, secretly, for respect to the superstitions of the sailors. Through her efforts the bodies of eighty four men killed at Gettysburg were returned home to lie in their native soil at Magnolia, eight years after their deaths.

The dead from Gettysburg were reinterred in a special ceremony on May 10, 1871. Six thousand people attended the services. Lt. Gen. Richard H. Anderson opened the occasion by introducing Rev. Ellison Capers, who read a prayer composed by Dr. John Bachman. He was present but too infirm to read it himself. He asked those present to emulate their Confederate ancestors' patriotic love of country and to learn here the lesson of mortality: to live their lives in such a way that they would someday be worthy of being reunited with these men. He prayed for the families and that the Southland would soon prosper again. The pupils of the Confederate Widows' Home sang an ode, assisted by a male choir.

Rev. John Girardeau, who had spoken at the first Magnolia Cemetery service, gave this address:

> The circumstances which assemble us in the streets of this City of the Dead are, in the last degree, solemn, tender and affecting. The bones of our brethren have for nearly eight years been sleeping in the graves in which they were laid on the bloody battlefield of Gettysburg. The wounded who survived for a brief while the carnage of that day, turned amid their last thoughts on earth to the State they had loved so well,

and before they yielded up their gallant spirits breathed the fervent entreaty 'Send our bodies to South Carolina to be buried there!' Was it that in their last moments of consciousness they recoiled from the thought that they would be interred in an enemy's soil, and that their graves would be designated as those of rebels and traitors? They were correct. When the Federal remains were carefully collected and buried with honor, the Confederates were left to sleep apart. But they will no longer sleep alone. They will now have a fellowship in death from which they have hitherto been excommunicated. Their dying wish is fulfilled. Their isolated repose has been interrupted by the gentle hands of their country women who have tenderly removed them from alien graves, and brought them hither for admission to the communion of kindred dead. They have come home at last; and we, their brethren, their comrades, bone of their bone and flesh of their flesh, are met with one accord to welcome them to their native soil. Shoulder to shoulder they stood; now let them lie side by side. Confederates in life, Confederates let them be in death. We are now standing by the open graves of those who died for liberty, who died for us. But enough! The mournful office which has summoned us hither waits to be performed.

The address was followed by a poem composed for the occasion after which the choir sang the "Ode Upon the Return of the Gettysburg Dead." While this was sung, the new graves were filled and all the graves then decorated with wreaths and floral crosses by the ladies. In the center of the burial ground, where the monument now stands, a large evergreen cross stood on a raised mound, crowned with white lilies. It bore this inscription: "In Memoriam—R.E. Lee."

On this day plans began for the headstones and future monument. Money was too scarce at the time to complete this project.

The South Carolina Legislature gave $1,000.00 towards the stones and promised a quantity of granite and marble then lying in Columbia, left over from rebuilding the state house burned by Sherman's forces. But before the Ladies' Memorial Association could have the stone hauled to Charleston, the government changed hands into the Reconstruction occupation government.

Once again, Mrs. Snowden found herself personally involved. She went to Columbia and came home with enough material to cut more than eight hundred headstones. She oversaw these being placed, as well as the granite base which forms the pedestal of the monument. The granite monument was completed in 1872, but eight more years would pass before the bronze figure of a Confederate soldier took his rightful place at the top.

Several bronze tablets were added as late as 1902, including one to honor the memory of Mary Amarinthia Yates Snowden, who died in 1898, and who had cared so much for the Confederate dead, providing this beautiful place for their final resting place.

Many Confederate veterans walked in the procession for Mary Amarinthia Snowden's funeral, held at the Huguenot Church in Charleston. She was then laid to rest in her beloved Magnolia Cemetery.

An article in the *Southern Christian Advocate* of March 3, 1898 described her well:

> Mrs. Snowden was a remarkable woman, and she rendered very great service. A Southerner of Southerners, a Confederate of Confederates, she devoted her life to distinctively Southern and Confederate ideas. The monument to Calhoun, the Ladies' Memorial Association, the Confederate section in Magnolia Cemetery, with its hero dead, the Confederate Home and School, all speak eloquently of the thoughts that ruled a brave, loving and unchangeable heart. This consecration of purpose made possible the large results of her endeavor. Such character and life as Mrs. Snowden's should be held

before the generations as an inspiration and an example. Mrs. Snowden was the incarnation of Southern womanhood in the War Between the States and after.

Mary Amarinthia Yates Snowden

BIBLIOGRAPHY

Charleston Courier. June 18, 1866.

Holmes, James G. editor. *Memorials to the Memory of Mrs. Mary Amarinthia Snowden* (Walker, Evans and Cogswell Co., 1898).

Mazyck, William G. Ladies' Memorial Association. *Confederate Memorial Day at Charleston, S.C., May 10, 1871.*

The *News and Courier*, May 10, 1916.

Year Book. City of Charleston, S.C., 1885.

Relics and records of the Confederate Museum, Charleston, S.C.

10

SERVANTS OF GOD AND MAN
The Sisters of Mercy

By
James A. Buttimer[1]

The political and social upheaval culminating in the American Civil War transformed not only the power structure of American society, but also the individual lives of millions of Americans. Much that had been commonplace prior to the war simply disappeared or was reduced to a shadow of its former significance at the war's end. The emancipation of the slaves and the dissolution of the slavocracy highlighted the most notable transformation of the past. Yet another momentous change occurred that took generations to fully appreciate. For three decades prior to the war, sectarian violence commingled with anti-immigrant hatred, convulsed American political and social life from Boston to New Orleans. In that timespan a tidal wave of the most wretchedly poor, degraded, and uneducated Catholics, the vast majority Irish, engulfed the seaboard cities of Protestant America, thereby knocking the legs of the social underpinning of American society asunder. Poor houses, jails, mental asylums, and pauper wards became the refuge of these strangers, many of whom spoke little or no English and possessed no marketable skills but raw labor. Even the most tolerant and sympathetic Americans recoiled in shock from the violence, alcoholism, and staggering mortality from disease attendant upon these foreigners. In some quarters the reaction against this class included violence from ad hoc groups of anti-Irish, anti-Catholic, and anti-immigrant organizations. So hot was the violence through the late 1850s that many Americans concluded that the war had as many sectarian as political roots of conflict. Abolitionists succeeded in crystallizing this thought in the minds of many Catholics by their insistence that these depraved Romish foreigners constituted proof that slavery and Catholicism were synonymous.[2]

Beginning in Massachusetts in the 1830s, sectarian violence claimed Catholic lives and property on a scale unimaginable only a few years before. Yet in the wake of the Civil War this violence dissipated so completely that the country never saw its like again. Many historians contend that Irish and Catholic soldiers in both armies so proved their worth to their respective societies that all but the most inveterate bigots accepted them as part of American society. Undoubtedly this view has merit. But as the study of the war itself grew from the political and military emphasis to the broader appreciation encompassing the social and personal experiences of those who lived it, another somewhat neglected explanation emerged to explain the dramatic reduction of bigotry: the role of Catholic religious orders in defusing prejudice. In diaries, letters, and testimonials of former prisoners-of-war, a resounding record of gratitude and awe testifies to the courage and devotion of religious women on battlefields, in hospitals, and on the home front throughout the deadly conflict. Protestant America, so suspicious of Catholic liturgy and teachings, invariably found nothing but praise for the acts of mercy performed by religious orders. The effects of religious orders in the South had even greater impact due to the relatively restricted roles of women in Southern society.

However well thought of after the war, religious orders in the South experienced a complex and sometimes contradictory relationship with Southerners. The education of poor Irish children and the order produced in the chaotic ghettoes in which they lived constituted an important service that garnered praise for Catholic sisters from largely Protestant communities. The Sisters of Charity in New Orleans and Vicksburg's Sisters of Mercy worked strenuously to mitigate the ills afflicting the Irish working on the levees near the Mississippi. The sisters in Vicksburg planted a screen of shrubbery to shield their orphanage and school from residents offended by the sight of the Irish children of the levees. Likewise, sisterhoods in Richmond, Charleston, Savannah, and Mobile attempted to provide services for the crush of famine-era immigrants often in poor health and with little means to adjust to the vagaries of the climate or shifting job market. Protestant mayors and city councils generally welcomed the order a religious community brought to the poorest of their inhabitants. Sometimes, though, this depended on what faction held political power. Upon the election of the Know-Nothing slate in the mayoral election of 1854 in Mobile, Alabama, the City Council fired the Sisters of Charity from their administration of City Hospital. This action followed only two years after the previous City Council invited the order to run the hospital, and a year after a catastrophic yellow fever epidemic struck the city in which the sisters in the hospital bore the greatest burdens in relieving the city of its distress. In 1855 the Sisters of Our Lady of Mercy in Columbia, South Carolina, withstood accusations from nativists that they extorted money from locals to support Catholic candidates for public office. Catholic sisters in New Orleans witnessed the most violent and protracted campaign against Catholics in the South from 1854-56 as nativist gangs resorted to beatings and assassinations against many prominent Irish Catholics including the heavily Irish police force. In general, though, Catholics were tolerated with much less violence in the South than the North. This led to pro-southern sympathies among many of the clergy and religious at the outbreak of the war.[3]

An interesting example of such an order was the Sisters of Our Lady of Mercy based in the diocesan centers of South Carolina and Georgia. Organized in 1829 by Bishop John England in Charleston, South Carolina, the order expanded to Savannah, Georgia in 1845 and Augusta in 1853. England condemned slavery, but perceived a greater threat from the violence propagated by abolitionists against Irish Catholics. He resolutely condemned abolitionists as violent radicals bent on the destruction of American society. In 1834 England returned to Charleston from a recruiting trip to Ireland for religious women for his diocese. He successfully returned with a contingent of Ursuline nuns from Blackrock convent in Cork along with two lay women who wished to join the Sisters of Our Lady of Mercy. While nearing Philadelphia, the ship was apprised of the burning of an Ursuline convent in Charlestowne, Massachusetts by a nativist mob excited by the abolitionist and nativist Lyman Beecher. The violence quickly spread along the mid-Atlantic seaboard, and England feared for the safety of his party to land in Charleston, South Carolina. However, the Mayor and City Council, along with many of the leading Protestants of Charleston, pledged to

defend the sisters against violence and the objections of a few prominent nativists who urged their rejection. This initial experience of
hatred and violence against Catholics in the North compared to the
relative tolerance accorded them in the South, remained imprinted
on the women who witnessed it. The two lay postulants in tow with
England and the Ursulines, became the founders of the order in
Georgia and its leaders for its first 25 years.[4]

Subsequently, even though they became the first white religious order to reject slavery in their rule, the sisters embraced the
South and its greater tolerance of Catholics. When war broke out in
1861, the sisters in Savannah remained steadfast in their support of
the South. At their commencement exercises in 1861-62, the girls of
St. Vincent's Academy in Savannah performed a dialogue entitled
"Secession Conference" which featured girls representing each state
that had formed the Confederacy. The Rev. Jeremiah O'Neill
crowned Mary Reilly as South Carolina, who in turn "called upon
her sisters to break the links that bind them to the old Union." Each
girl representing a southern state accepted a crown in turn. The song
"Maryland, My Maryland" was included in 1862 in hopes that the
state that was home to the first independent American order, Mother
Seton's Sisters of Charity, might join in secession. The fervor impart-
ed in the drama produced a blend of religious and national sympathies reflected in the fact that six of the twelve girls participating in
the pageant themselves joined the order. Seven of the first nine grad-
uates of St. Vincent's Academy entered the sisterhood in the 1860s.
At the war's end the sisters went to the aid of Mrs. Jefferson Davis
under house arrest in Savannah, enrolling her daughter, Winnie, in
St. Vincent's Academy and instructing young Jeff in prayer on his
daily trips to the convent.[5]

Nativist elements of the Union army had the further effect of
aiding southern Catholics in their loyalty to the South. Union troops
evacuating Jacksonville, Florida in March 1863 looted the Church of
the Immaculate Conception of its sacred vessels before burning the
structure to the ground. Offenses like this often occurred in the
absence of heavily Irish or Catholic regiments to prevent them.
Following Sherman's capture of Jackson, Mississippi in July 1863, the

Catholic church in town suffered desecration and burning following the removal of Irish companies in Sherman's command from its vicinity. Twice more the structures that substituted for the Church suffered the same fate from the same army. When an Irish woman was asked why only the Catholic churches were destroyed and not the Protestant, she replied "When the divil sends his immissaries, sure he always takes care of his own." Even sisters belonging to orders originating in the North and performing services in Northern hospitals suffered depredations at the hands of nativist Union generals. Recent transplants from their Pittsburgh, Pennsylvania motherhouse, the Sisters of Mercy in Vicksburg included Sister Ignatius Sumner, the niece of abolitionist Charles Sumner. This order staffed the Washington Infirmary, and after it burned, Douglas Hospital in Washington, DC during the war with 22 sisters in attendance. Yet this meant little to General Henry W. Slocum of New York, whose uncle had harbored the notorious "Maria Monk" who penned a scandalous false biography, supposedly bringing to light atrocities committed in an enclosed order in the 1830's.Slocum used the convent of the Vicksburg branch-house as his quarters, refusing to relinquish the house until commanded to do so by Secretary of War Stanton. Slocum further displayed his resentment at being forced to accommodate the sisters by denying their request to provide rations for the orphans of Natchez.[6]

Although individual soldiers or isolated commanders furthered the prewar violence against Catholics, the vast majority of soldiers in both armies recognized the extraordinary commitment of religious orders to serve suffering humanity. Many were humbled by the unflagging courage displayed by sisters on the battlefield. At the battle of Galveston a wounded rebel noticed a group of women rushing to the aid of wounded over ground "thick with bullets." Exclaiming to a friend that they would all be killed his companion casually replied "Oh, those are the Sisters. They are looking for the wounded. They're not afraid of anything." During the siege of Vicksburg, while residents retired to caves to withstand the Union artillery, the Sisters of Mercy traveled through the blasted city streets to nurse wounded in the vacant houses still standing. The only admonition the bishop offered to these sisters was not to "go out altogether, for I do not want all of you to be killed."[7]

By far the most profound appreciation of religious orders occurred in hospitals, whether in formal structures away from front lines or in tented field hospitals. Initially, prior to 1840, the earliest practitioners of nursing came from southern religious orders. However, the wave of famine-era Irish immigrants coupled with a sizable German Catholic migration after 1848, altered the growth of hospitals and nursing orders to the North in consequence of the vast majority of emigrants settling there. From 1840-1870 religious orders in the North initiated a precipitous rise in construction of local hospitals while growth in the South stagnated. At the outbreak of war Catholic sisters constituted the only group with a degree of nursing skills in both the North and the South. Epidemics of typhus, cholera, smallpox, and especially yellow fever provided Catholic sisters in the South opportunities to relieve suffering and gain nursing skills. Primarily, epidemics remained an urban phenomenon, and the prestige of religious orders ran high in southern cities. The countryside remained suspicious and sometimes hostile to Catholics. The Civil War brought many Southerners who had never met a Catholic into contact with religious orders for the first time. The results were often outlandish. When five Sisters of Charity arrived in Marietta, Georgia in February 1863, locals accosted them as they awaited transportation, musing "What or who are they?" with some pushing roughly against them to determine if they were human. When a sister spoke to the group, they clapped their hands, shouting "She spoke! She spoke!"[8]

The success of Catholic religious orders in nursing and hospital administration centers on four major factors, according to Sister Mary Denis Maher: the tradition of nursing the sick in Europe dating back to the Middle Ages; the advocacy of Florence Nightingale and others who stressed that sisters possessed the essential combination of nursing skills and religious commitment; the flexibility and pragmatism of American orders that responded to a variety of exigencies; and the written regulations, or rules, structuring religious life that served as a training manual on how patients should be treated. The preeminence of religious orders in hospitals of the South became even more pronounced than in the North because of widespread prejudice against women assuming public roles in southern society, with many Southern women facing censure and ridicule for accepting positions considered lowly. Prior to the war nursing had been a primarily male, disreputable occupation with poor houses and pauper wards often employing patients to save money. In concert with the prevailing attitudes associated with the "cult of domesticity" emphasizing the essential role of women in the home as wives and mothers, these circumstances combined to form a barrier to many women who otherwise thought the work noble. Lay women who worked in Confederate hospitals often regarded with scorn those women who let their self-respect interfere with duty to the suffering. Kate Cumming, who nursed at several hospitals with the Army of Tennessee, assigned blame to southern women in the face of defeat for not supporting their men. She further drew a direct comparison between southern lay women and religious when she observed "It seems strange that they can do with honor what is wrong for other Christian women to do."[9]

Cumming admired the flexible utility of sisterhoods such as Mobile's Sisters of Charity in Canty Hospital, noting "Here one of them is a druggist; another acts the part of a steward; and, in fact, they could take charge of the whole hospital, with the exception of the medical department." Protestant ministers also noted the contrast between secular women and Catholic sisters. The Rev. Charles Todd Quintard advocated the formation of sisterhoods in the Episcopal church to impart discipline and medical training to Protestant women. Cumming herself patently emulated the examples of Catholic sisters she encountered, proclaiming "Mrs. Williamson and I live like Sisters of Charity; we get up at four in the morning and breakfast by candlelight" before preparing breakfast for the invalids, writing letters for the men, or mending articles of clothing for them. Mary Chestnut in Virginia cited the enhanced care of wounded by the Sisters of Charity in Richmond following the first battle of Manassas. "Everything was so clean-and in perfect order...In that hospital with the Sisters of Charity [the Yankee prisoners] were better off than our own men at the other [Confederate] hospitals."[10]

The Confederate government recognized the superior care of wounded under lay and religious women and took steps to formalize their vital role in hospitals in the passage of an act of the Confederate Congress in September 1862. This law established positions in hospitals for matrons, assistant matrons, nurses, cooks, and ward masters "giving preferences in all cases to females where their services may best subserve the purpose." The passage of this act did not magically make all prejudice against women in hospitals disappear. Some doctors reacted against certain types of women deemed unsuited for the work. These women had unreal expectations for their own comfort, sometimes demanding private quarters and rations superior to those given the sick and wounded. Consequently, some authorities restricted access to lay women thought lacking in the essential selflessness inherent in religious orders. Medical Director of the Army of Tennessee, Samuel H. Stout, earned a reputation for scorning lay women in favor of Catholic sisters. But as he explained to Kate Cumming, that was a view he espoused early in the war when ladies in Nashville so interfered with the work in his wards that he banned them from the hospital.He later relented when he saw the dedication of lay women devoted to relieving suffering in the same spirit as religious women. Yet even matrons such as Cumming, who recognized the desperate need for women in the hospitals, also realized the liabilities of lay women lacking the discipline of religious orders. After observing a group of women preparing to leave one hospital creating a vexing and noisy disruption looking for their belongings, Cumming wrote "I thought it was not strange that surgeons should prefer Sisters of Charity to nurse their sick, for they know how to keep quiet." To understand the intense focus and enhanced care widely attributed to religious orders over that accorded most lay women, one can understand the basis of such an observation by examining the rules of sisterhoods. In writing the rule of the Sisters of Our Lady of Mercy, who formed the majority of all religious women in the Carolinas and Georgia, Bishop John England insisted that sisters obey doctors and hospital administrators to the same extent as they would their ecclesiastical superiors:

> Should the Sisters have employment in any Hospital
> or Charitable or Religious Institution, they shall pay

great respect to the Administrators, or Governors, or Physicians who might have any charge therein, and shall obey them in every lawful direction which they might give. In particular, they shall never interfere therewith—and they shall manage the Property intrusted (sic) to them as they shall render an account to Our Lord Jesus Christ.[11]

While religious orders appeared to provide doctors with an ideal cadre of conscientious nurses, in some cases they still had to overcome prejudice in Confederate hospitals. The Convent of Our Lady of Mercy in Charleston, South Carolina acceded to a request from Bishop McGill of Richmond, Virginia and the Confederate War Department in December 1861 to administer a hospital at White Sulphur Springs in western Virginia. The hospital and the sisters relocated to Montgomery White Sulphur Springs in May 1862 due to pressure from Union forces. There they encountered opposition from Protestant doctors and local ministers who chafed at "the Catholic influence." Particularly incensed when the sisters' chaplain was designated as Chaplain of the Post, the offended parties charged that the sisters denied access to Protestant ministers in order to baptize Protestant soldiers. Sister De Sales Brennan denied obstructing access to ministers but offered another view of the situation: "The fact is that they are frantic at the influence we have over the men and at the number that have been baptized." The wounded feelings among offended doctors and ministers festered into organized resistance against the presence of the sisters. During a smallpox outbreak in January 1863, four physicians refused to enter the quarantine house at the hospital. Sister De Sales, who had already assigned one sister to the house, viewed their refusal to serve as cowardice in the face of duty. The surgeons, though, answered that their refusal was in protest "because of favoritism shown and authority given to a religious party placed in the Hospital who are permitted to have control of everything." Eventually, those who resented the backing of the sisters by Post Surgeon J. Lewis Woodville, brought formal charges against him resulting in a court martial trial in April 1864. The court exonerated Woodville "who has been most vexatiously harassed and grossly calumniated by charges for which there is not the slightest warrant..."

Woodville stated in closing testimony that the basis for all the consternation derived from:

> "a settled purpose in certain quarters to drive from this Hospital these humane and most useful Sisters of Mercy who have been of such essential importance to its proper management, and whose kind attentions have contributed so much to the comfort of the patients. This purpose, originating I presume in some narrow-minded sectarian prejudices, was manifested in various efforts to make the situation of these sisters as uncomfortable as possible; and before any degree of harmony could be re-established, two Ministers of the Gospel, four contract physicians, one assistant surgeon and one Quarter Master (all of religious sects other than the sisters) had to be relieved of duty here—two of the prosecutors, ... being two of the parties so relieved."[12]

While prejudice made the lives of some sisters uncomfortable, a more deadly threat to their health arose from exposure to disease and exhaustion from overwork in the hospitals. Sister De Sales Brennan contracted erysipelas from soldiers stationed at the hospital in Virginia, and all five of the sisters stationed there contracted and survived smallpox. No definitive totals of sisters dying in hospitals are available mainly because their work at the time was so urgent that few religious communities were able to chronicle events related to the personal health of their members. The sheer scope of the workload attending the sick and wounded contributed to a deteriorating state of health for sisters in hospitals. The Vicksburg Sisters of Mercy accompanied Confederate wounded in boxcars from Meridian to Demopolis to Selma and finally Shelby Springs in Alabama. After enduring the siege of Vicksburg, the sisters then suffered the bombardment of

Jackson, which destroyed one of the wards of their makeshift hospital. They then hastily prepared the wounded for evacuation "feeling every moment would be their last." Sleepless nights and hunger accompanied them as they moved fitfully, occasionally "boiling water by the side of the road." Exhausted, with one sister suffering from jaundice and exposure, they found themselves "on half rations until the sick came, the dirt, being as usual in melancholy ascendancy...." Nevertheless, they attended to casualties and the sick while cleaning the premises of their new hospital site.Sister Agatha MacNamara wrote from western Virginia in the fall of 1863 to Bishop Lynch back home in Charleston of the stress entailed with treating large numbers of wounded hastily brought to the hospital at White Sulphur Springs: "You may well imagine how trying it was for us to have so large a crowd of badly wounded men ushered in upon us without a moment's warning. The wounded were brought on litters and left before my ward until my heart grew sick and I was compelled to whisper to myself again and again ... 'Take it easy'."[13]

The war played havoc upon the branch-houses and foundations of religious communities, often splitting sisterhoods into isolated bands with some departing for hospital work in distant locations while others attended orphans and boarders in their care. At the war's end the Sisters of Our Lady of Mercy from Charleston found their community "like Caesar's Gaul, divided into three parts": a contingent remained in Charleston staffing a hospital and tending prisoners; another group having to find their way home from the hospital in Montgomery White Sulphur Springs, Virginia; and the rest caring for orphans and boarders removed during the siege of Charleston to Sumter, South Carolina. Sisters such as the last group also faced privations, denying their own needs while caring for children. Bishop Augustin Verot wrote Archbishop Spaulding in March 1865 that the sisters in Savannah with forty-five girls in their care "were on the brink of starvation." The records of the sisterhood reveal the extent of the depredations of their community. The 1860s witnessed the deaths of over twenty percent of their members—nine of forty-three women. No other decade of the nineteenth century approached the mortality of the war and Reconstruction. The loss of these sisters surpassed the entire total incurred by the order in three major yellow fever epidemics. Their constancy and devotion resided in the hearts of a grateful city for generations. Seventy-two years later at the dedication of the new St. Mary's Home for girls, John Gleason related how the sisters went without food at this time to feed the girls in their care. Undoubtedly, this factored in the high mortality rate of the sisterhood.[14]

Other voices joined the chorus of praise of Catholic sisters in the wake of the war. Many came from former prisoners who received comfort from religious orders. So many vivid and moving testimonials from former Union soldiers flooded Congress in support of reparations for the Sisters of Our Lady of Mercy in Charleston, that the sisters eventually received $12,000 in 1871 to rebuild the orphanage destroyed during the siege of that city. Letter after letter extolled the sacrifices of these women in aiding Union prisoners, including black soldiers of the 54th Massachusetts captured after their assault on Battery Wagener. The South Carolina legislature included these letters in a petition to the federal government for reparations, including one from a former Union officer who credited the work of the sisters in saving the lives of many of his men: "I am not of your Church and have always been taught to believe it to be nothing but evil; however, actions speak louder than words, and I am free to admit that if Christianity does exist on the earth, it has some of its closest followers among the ladies of your Order." Confederate soldiers in northern hospitals received similar care when allowed. One prisoner in Alton, Illinois became so impressed by the Daughters of Charity who visited the prison that he requested to be baptized as a Catholic. The priest who arrived to perform the service relinquished his normal authority as the Southerner[14] refused to be baptized by anyone but one of the sisters who attended him. His wish was granted. So it was that many soldiers ignorant of Catholic liturgy or beliefs, but humbled by the acts of mercy by Catholic sisters, requested to join "the religion of the sisters."[15]

Perhaps the most profound measure of the impact of religious orders in the South resided in the hearts of Protestants who did not feel compelled to embrace Catholicism as their own religion, but who nevertheless strove to honor the example of tolerance and generosity learned at the hands of religious women. Wounded in the foot at Chickamauga, Bill Fletcher of the Fifth Texas Infantry arrived with his gangrenous wound days later in the Third Georgia Hospital in Augusta staffed by the Sisters of Our Lady of Mercy. There Fletcher, who had been raised to believe "there was no place in heaven for a Catholic," encountered the Irish immigrant sisters for the first time. As he declared in his memoir years later, "I was in love with the women and the uniform at once and have not gotten over it yet." Exhausted surgeons wanted to amputate his leg, but Fletcher begged an attempt to save it. He later credited the sisters in charge of dressing the wound with saving his leg. Following the war Fletcher returned to Texas, and though not formally educated, he became one of the richest men in the state by the turn of the century. He developed some of the first technology for industrial logging and sawmills in America and exported the first shipment of yellow pine in the nation. The first phone lines in Texas ran between two of his mills. Wishing to pay a debt of gratitude to the Catholic sisters who saved his leg, Fletcher contacted the Sisters of Charity in Galveston and told them of his plans to build a hospital for their branch-house in Beaumont. Fletcher donated the land as well as the lumber used to construct the hospital. During construction he ignored the loud and public censure from Protestant preachers who castigated "an influential man who did much harm in what they called his influence against Christianity." This hospital, the Hotel Dieu of Beaumont, became the primary health care facility for east Texas and west Louisiana at a time when none existed. Furthermore, Fletcher instructed his children to assist the sisters following his death. Each Christmas they traveled with donations in cash, food, and clothing for the sisters' foundations at their hospital and orphanage. Thus did the kindness and devotion of Catholic sisters in Georgia take root and blossom miles and years removed in the face of continued prejudice.[16]

Bill Fletcher represents an extraordinary example of what Protestants in the South gave back in honor of the sacrifice of Catholic sisters during the war. The religious order that tended his wounds benefited in other ways as did the Catholics of Georgia.

After the war abolitionist congregations flooded the state and brought with them their old hatred of Catholics. But while northern, abolitionist papers like the Methodist Advocate in Macon attacked Catholics in general and the foundations of the Sisters of Our Lady of Mercy, southern Methodists and doctors of other Protestant sects advocated turning the administration of Augusta's City Hospital over to the religious order. Within ten years this order expanded hospitals in Savannah and Atlanta to become the largest single provider of health care services in nineteenth-century Georgia, while representing only one percent of the statewide population that was Irish Catholic.[17]

Bishop Augustin Verot of Savannah correctly surmised the impact of the war and the changes it portended among Protestant opinion of Catholics when he wrote "A good number of crackers have seen our priests and our Sisters of Charity for the first time in their lives... and they could not but carry away a very favorable impression of what they saw with their own eyes." What they carried away enabled Catholics throughout the nation to be integrated into the social fabric as never before. The Catholic Church finally had what it needed most—champions among rank and file Protestants who returned to their communities and carried with them, like Bill Fletcher, memories of devoted Catholic sisters that stayed with them the rest of their lives. These memories enabled individuals to stand like Fletcher against prejudice directed at Catholics and their institutions. Most veterans did not have the means of Fletcher to proclaim their gratitude on such a magnificent scale. Nevertheless, they expressed their admiration for the sacrifice of Catholic sisters, often with a simplicity of grandeur. Upon the death of a Sister of Our Lady of Mercy in Charleston in 1887, of all the accolades and gifts bestowed in her honor "the most touching tribute of all was that of an old Confederate soldier who sent a garland of hay and wheat to the Academy of Our Lady of Mercy in remembrance of Sister M. Xavier Dunn's patient and arduous work in the Confederate hospitals."

William A. Fletcher
Fletcher credited the Sisters of Mercy with
saving his life. It changed his attitude towards
Catholics forever.

The Hotel Dieu in Beaumont, Texas. It was started by William
Fletcher in 1897.

The Sisters of Our Lady of Mercy in Savannah, Georgia, c. 1872. They staffed the 3rd Georgia Hospital in Augusta that Fletcher credited with saving his life. Most of these women were Irish born. Part of their appeal lay in the fact that their habits were black, making them appear similar to the many women in mourning throughout the South.

Notes

[1] James A. Buttimer, "By Their Deeds You Shall Know Them: The Sisters of Our Lady of Mercy in Georgia 1845-1893" (M.A. thesis, Armstrong Atlantic State University, 1996).

[2] Ray Allen Billington's *The Protestant Crusade, 1800-1860: A Study of the Origins of American Nativism* (New York: The Macmillan Company, 1938) remains the preeminent source documenting the antagonisms and violence associated with this time period. Hasia Diner's Erin's Daughters in America, Irish Immigrant Women in the Nineteenth Century (Baltimore: Johns Hopkins University Press, 1983) highlights the pivotal role of Irish women both in religious orders and in the secular work place, although her sources derive primarily from northern communities.

[3] See Earl F. Niehaus, *The Irish in New Orleans 1800-1860* (Louisiana State University Press: Baton Rouge, 1965), 82 and Sister M. Paulinus Oakes, R.S.M, *Angels of Mercy: An Eyewitness Account of the Civil War and Yellow Fever* (: Baltimore:Cathedral Foundation Press, 1998), 42-3, 51-3, 78-9 for the work of Catholic sisters with the children of the levees. James A. Buttimer, "By Their Deeds You Shall Know Them: The Sisters of Our Lady of Mercy in Georgia 1845-1893" (M.A. thesis, Armstrong Atlantic State University, 1999), 59-60 concerning the Sisters of Charity in Mobile and the Sisters of Our Lady of Mercy in Columbia.

[4] On the burning of the Ursuline Convent and the spread of violence, see Billington, *The Protestant Crusade*, 89-90. For comments on the voyage of Bishop England, see Sister Ann Francis Campbell, O.L.M., "Bishop England's Sisterhood, 1829-1929" (Ph.D. diss., St. Louis University, 1968), 34. On the two women who became the leaders of the Georgia sisterhood, see Buttimer, "By Their Deeds You Shall Know Them", 14-15.

[5] Buttimer, "By Their Deeds You Shall Know Them", 64-5, 68-9. On the destruction of the church in Jacksonville, see Michael V. Gannon, *Rebel Bishop: The Life and Era of Augustin Verot* (Milwaukee: The Bruce

Publishing Company, 1964), 71-72, 110-114. For the Vicksburg Sisters of Mercy, see Oakes, *Angels of Mercy*, 22-23, 30-32.

[6] Michael Fitzpatrick, "The Mercy Brigade: Roman Catholic Nuns in the Civil War", *Civil War Times* (October 1997), 34, 39. This is an interesting article with references often not cited elsewhere. Fitzpatrick took five years to research the article, although it is not documented entirely. Also see Oakes, *Angels of Mercy*, 16.

[7] For information on the development of nursing and hospital administration among American religious orders, see Ann Doyle, R.N., "Nursing by Religious Orders in the United States", *The American Journal of Nursing*, "Part One, 1809-1840" (July 1929), 775-785; and "Part Two, 1841-1870" (August 1929), 959-969. On the reaction of citizens in Marietta, see *Annals of the Civil War of the Sisters of Charity*, 215-222, Archives of St. Joseph's Provincial House, Emmitsburg, Md.

[8] Sister Mary Denis Maher, *To Bind Up the Wounds: Catholic Sister Nurses in the U.S. Civil War* (New York: Greenwood Press, 1989), 39. On the prejudice against women in hospitals, see H.H. Cunningham, *Doctors in Gray, the Confederate Medical Service* (Baton Rouge: Louisiana State University Press, 1958), 73. Also see *Kate Cumming, Kate: the Journal of a Confederate Nurse*, Richard Harwell, ed. (Baton Rouge: Louisiana State University Press, 1959), 123-4, 163, 176, 237, 273.

[9] Cumming, *Journal of a Confederate Nurse*, 83, 101. Quote by Mary Chestnut from Fitzpatrick, The Mercy Brigade, 36

[10] On the act of the Confederate Congress, see Cunningham, 73. See Maher, *To Bind Up the Wounds*, 56-58, for a description of the unsuitability's of some women in hospitals. On Stout's attitudes toward women, see Cumming,113-14; the quote from Cumming is on page 10. The last quote is from the Rules for the Sisters of Our Lady of Mercy in Savannah, 84, Archives of the Convent of St. Vincent de Paul, Savannah. Many if not most of the American religious orders at the time probably had very similar rules for the sick as most borrowed heavily from the rule of the Sisters of Charity in Emmitsburg. Their rule was based on that authored by Vincent de Paul for the

Daughters of Charity in France hundreds of years earlier. This reflected an activist ministry outside of convent walls with charity toward the poor and visiting the sick in their homes.

[11] Campbell, "Bishop England's Sisterhood", 96-121, 137-39.

[12] Maher, 119, 104; Oakes, *Angels of Mercy*, 23-4. Quote on the Charleston sisters is from Campbell, "Bishop England's Sisterhood", 152. The quote on the sisters in Savannah is from Gannon, Rebel Bishop, 147. The mortality of the sisters in Savannah and the dedication of St. Mary's Home for Girls is in Buttimer, "By Their Deeds You Shall Know Them", 68.

[13] Maher, *To Bind Up the Wounds*, 149, 118, 139.

[14] William A. Fletcher, *Rebel Private Front and Rear: Memoirs of a Confederate Soldier* (New York: Penguin Books, 1995), 103-106 for a description of his treatment in Augusta. For his actions after the war including his building of the hospital in Beaumont see the Afterword by his great-granddaughter, Vallie Fletcher Taylor, 215-23.

[15] Buttimer, "By Their Deeds You Shall Know Them", 77.

[16] Gannon, *Rebel Bishop*, 148; Campbell, "Bishop England's Sisterhood", 235.

[17] Ibid.

BIBLIOGRAPHY

Archives of the Convent of St. Vincent de Paul and St. Vincent's Academy, Savannah, Georgia. Rules for the Sisters of Our Lady of Mercy in Savannah, Georgia, Organized by the Right Rev. J. England, First Bishop of Charleston, in 1829, and Modified in 1835, 1837, 1844, and 1869.

Archives of the Daughters of Charity, St. Joseph's Provincial House, Emmitsburg, Maryland. Annals of the Civil War.

Billington, Ray Allen. *The Protestant Crusade, 1800-1860: A Study of the Origins of American Nativism.* New York: The Macmillan Company, 1938.

Buttimer, James A. "By Their Deeds You Shall Know Them: The Sisters of Our Lady of Mercy in Georgia, 1845-1893". M.A. thesis, Armstrong Atlantic State University, 1999.

Campbell, Sister Anne Francis, O.L.M. "Bishop England's Sisterhood, 1829-1929". Ph.D. dissertation, St. Louis University, 1968.

Cumming, Kate. *Kate: The Journal of a Confederate Nurse.* Richard Harwell, ed. Baton Rouge: Louisiana State University Press, 1959.

Cunningham, H.H. *Doctors in Gray, the Confederate Medical Service.* Baton Rouge: Louisiana State University Press, 1958.

Doyle, Ann, R.N. "Nursing by Religious Orders in the United States". *American Journal of Nursing* (July-December, 1929): 775-875; 959-969; 1085-1095; 1197-1207; 1331-1343; 1464-1484.

Fitzpatrick, Michael. "The Mercy Brigade: Roman Catholic Nuns in the Civil War". *Civil War Times* (October, 1997), 34-40.

Fletcher, William A. *Rebel Soldier Front and Rear: The Memoirs of a Confederate Soldier.* New York: Meridian Books, 1997.

Gannon, Michael V. *Rebel Bishop: The Life and Era of Augustin Verot.* Milwaukee: The Bruce Publishing Company, 1964.

Maher, Sister Mary Denis. *To Bind Up the Wounds: Catholic Sister Nurses in the U. S. Civil War.* New York: Greenwood Press, 1989.

Niehaus, Earl F. *The Irish in New Orleans, 1800-1860.* Baton Rouge: Louisiana State University Press, 1965.

Sumner, Sister Ignatius, R.S.M. *Angels of Mercy: An Eyewitness Account of the Civil War and Yellow Fever.* Mary Paulinus Oakes, ed., Baltimore: Cathedral Foundation Press, 1998.

ABOUT THE AUTHORS

Dr. Anne J. Bailey has written numerous books on the American Civil War, including *Portraits of Conflict: A Photographic History of Georgia in the Civil War* (1996); *Chessboard of War: Sherman and Hood in the Autumn Campaigns of 1864* (2000) and *War and Ruin: William T. Sherman and the Savannah Campaign* (2003). She is editor of the *Georgia Historical Quarterly*, and co-editor of the University of Nebraska's "Great Campaigns of the Civil War" series. She currently teaches at Georgia College and State University in Milledgeville, Georgia.

Dr. William H. Baria received his degree in medicine from Tulane University in 1944. A former newspaper columnist for the *Northside News*, he received the Hall-Rearick Award for Regional Fiction in 1996.

James A. Buttimer was raised in Savannah and received a Master's Degree with Honors in History from Armstrong Atlantic State University in 1999, his thesis being "By Their Deeds You Shall Know Them: The Sisters of Our Lady of Mercy in Georgia, 1845-93." He has written and co-produced a video, "Georgia's Sisters of Mercy" broadcast on Georgia Public Television in 2001. He has researched extensively Savannah's Irish community and has been Chairman of the Savannah Irish Festival since 1999. He is currently writing a novel based on the life of his Irish immigrant ancestor in nineteenth-century Savannah.

Jeanne M. Christie graduated from the University of Connecticut, and has worked on several projects with the National Park Service regarding the roles of women. Her published works include *Dear American: Letters Home From Vietnam, In a Combat Zone*, and *A Piece of My Heart* about women in Vietnam.

Barbara Duffey is a graduate of Johns Hopkins University, and author of *Banshees, Bugles and Belles: True Ghost Stories of Georgia* (1995), *Angels and Apparitions: True Ghost Stories from the South* (1997), and *Miracles* *from Heaven* (1998). She currently resides in Eatonton, Georgia and lectures on writing.

Mauriel Phillips Joslyn is a graduate of Mary Washington College and Georgia College and State University. She is author of *Immortal Captives: The Story of 600 Confederate Officers and the United States Prisoner of War Policy* (1996), and *Charlotte's Boys: The Civil War Correspondence of the Branch Family of Savannah* (1996), and editor of *A Meteor Shining Brightly: Essays on Maj. Gen. Patrick R. Cleburne* (1998). She has written numerous articles on Confederate history and Irish history topics.

Norma Jean Perkins received her Bachelor of Arts in History and Sociology from Mercer University. She is currently a free-lance writer and participant in War Between the States living history events. Norma's husband John is a member of the Sons of Confederate Veterans. They have three adult children and one very arrogant dog.

June Murray Wells is a native of Charleston, South Carolina and former Historian General of the United Daughters of the Confederacy. She served as President General of that organization from 1998-2000. Author of numerous articles on Confederate history and 1989 recipient of the Palmetto Award, she is director of the Confederate Museum in Charleston.

Julieanna Williams is a collector of 19th century jewelry and clothing. She researches and lectures on the life of women during the 1860's period. She and her husband Doug are participants of living history events and live in Mableton, Georgia.